LITTLE BOOK OF
BRITAIN AT WAR

LITTLE BOOK OF

BRITAIN AT WAR

First published in the UK in 2012

© Demand Media Limited 2012

www.demand-media.co.uk

Printed and bound in China

ISBN 978-1-909217-14-0

The views in this book are those of the author but they are general views only and readers are urged to consult the relevant and qualified specialist for individual advice in particular situations.

Demand Media Limited hereby exclude all liability to the extent permitted by law of any errors or omissions in this book and for any loss, damage or expense (whether direct or indirect) suffered by a third party relying on any information contained in this book.

All our best endeavours have been made to secure copyright clearance for every photograph used but in the event of any copyright owner being overlooked please address correspondence to Demand Media Limited, Unit D1, Fairoaks Airport, Chobham, Surrey, GU24 8HX

Contents

Introduction

It was approaching 11.15 on the morning of Sunday, 3 September 1939. Throughout the British Isles, families were clustered around their wireless sets, anxious to hear the latest news. But this was no ordinary Sunday morning, and the broadcast those families were about to hear contained no run-of-the-mill announcement.

The listeners drew closer to their wirelesses, and noisy children were hushed, as the measured tones of Neville Chamberlain cut clearly through the airwaves. But while the Prime Minister's voice remained steady, he was unable to provide his listeners with the reassuring news they had been hoping to hear. On the contrary, he made the announcement that the entire nation had been dreading: Britain was at war with Germany.

An ultimatum delivered to the German government by the British ambassador in Berlin, demanding the withdrawal of thousands of troops which had poured into Poland two days previously, had been ignored, Chamberlain informed his listeners. Now Britain and France were to honour their obligations and come to the aid of the Polish people. Adolf Hitler, Chamberlain noted grimly, could only be stopped by force.

Since the end of World War I in 1918, Britain's armed services had been active on many fronts, but this was different. The prospect of a long, drawn-out, bloody and costly conflict with Germany

and her allies was real, and those optimists who cried "It'll be over by Christmas", as older optimists had at the start of the Great War in 1914, were this time met with readily expressed scepticism. Britain faced hardship, tragedy, grief, privation and a thousand other cruel cuts before she could claim victory.

Chamberlain, referring to the uncertain future staring Britons in the face, felt confident enough in their steadfast natures to declare in his wireless announcement: "…now that we have resolved to finish it I know that you will play your part with calmness and courage." No statesman ever spoke a truer word.

Over the following six years, the

people of Britain were to display extraordinary levels of hard graft, fortitude and cool, calm, dogged determination as they faced a ruthless and formidable enemy. Ever since, in times of strife, Britons have evoked the Dunkirk spirit of the Bulldog Breed that was so evident during World War II.

And the efforts of Britons on the home front were to prove as important as those of the men on the front line. The country was facing a new kind of war – a war fought at home.

If Britain was dismayed by Chamberlain's announcement, she was also prepared. The coming war would place an almost unbearable strain on the country's economy and people, but the planners had been busy for years, and certain strategies for coping were already in place. Even the best planner struggles to prepare for the unknown, however. Some of the dangers to be faced, and some of the measures taken to ensure the country would survive, had never been encountered before. This time round, it was going to be different.

Britain had faced bombing raids mounted by aerial German forces before – World War I had seen the country

Left: Britons faced a ruthless and formidable enemy

Far Left: Chamberlain told listeners that Hitler could only be stopped by force

suffer more than 500 deaths as a result of raids by Zeppelin airships and Gotha bomber aircraft. But the intervening years had seen an immeasurable strengthening of the German air force and technical advances beyond imagination.

By 1939, the Nazis' Luftwaffe was a formidable foe, ready to reap a terrible revenge for the loss of World War I on Britain's towns and cities, her industrial and military strongholds and her people. The population would soon become used to the sound of sirens warning of the approach of enemy bombers and to the nightly retreat to the air raid shelter. Finding one's way in total darkness would become a precious skill as a strict blackout was enforced in an effort to blindfold German pilots.

Some urban areas were to find

WOMEN OF BRITAIN
COME INTO
THE FACTORIES

ASK AT ANY EMPLOYMENT EXCHANGE FOR ADVICE AND FULL DETAILS

themselves temporarily childless following the implementation of long-laid plans to evacuate children from vulnerable regions. Thousands of youngsters were to find themselves living rural lives they had never dreamt of.

While the armed services steeled themselves to resist Hitler's ferocious assaults, outwit him in the field and strike at the heart of his growing empire, on the home front the war effort was equally valiant. From the firewatchers warning of deadly conflagrations to the heroic ambulance drivers and fire crews, from the air raid wardens who patrolled the streets to the famed volunteers of Dad's Army – the Home Guard – thousands would be recognised for their courageous contribution.

The coming war would introduce other strange novelties to these islands. Leaving home without their outlandish-looking gas masks would become, for some, unthinkable. Posters and films shown in cinemas would urge Britons to be vigilant, to curb their instinct to gossip in case they were overheard by German spies, to scrimp, to save and to dig their gardens in support of the push for victory.

The war that was about to be

unleashed in September 1939 was also to bring about social upheaval on an unheard of scale. Class distinctions would start to blur as the realities of rationing of food, clothing, petrol and other commodities hit home. Every man, woman and child in the country, regardless of social status, would be affected.

Perhaps the most far-reaching change would come in the world of work. Who would man the factories producing vital arms, vehicles and materials now the nation's men were at war? Who would help to keep the country's farms productive when imports were threatened by enemy action on the high seas?

The answer was of course: Britain's women. World War II was to bring about a revolution in the way women contributed to the well-being of the nation and to the household.

Faced by danger, hunger, tragedy and sacrifice, home front Britain nevertheless kept smiling through, as it was urged to do by the Forces' Sweetheart, songstress Vera Lynn. Britain at war proved to be Britain at its best.

Out of Harm's Way

In a wartime poster, an Air Raid Precautions warden leans down towards a small boy who is kitted out in his own version of the ARP uniform and is clearly anxious to do his bit for the war effort. The grown-up warden wags his finger and advises sternly: "Leave this to us, sonny. *You* ought to be out of London."

This was a fictional small boy, created by the Ministry of Health to publicise its Evacuation Scheme and drawn by an artist. But many thousands of real, live children were given similar advice in the early days of World War II, and did indeed leave London. In fact, Britain has never experienced a greater mass movement of people than the evacuation process that started on 1 September 1939, the day German forces invaded Poland.

In all, Operation Pied Piper, as the first evacuation exercise was known, moved nearly 3.75 million people – adults as well as children, from London and many other locations – in the early part of the war. The idea was simple: people had to be shifted away from the places that were at greatest risk of bombardment by the Luftwaffe – in other words cities, towns, centres of industry and locations of military importance.

Plans for evacuation had been drawn up by the government as early as the summer of 1938, as the threat of war with Germany loomed ever larger, although preliminary planning had been

carried out much earlier, as soon as it became clear Hitler was not to be trusted and might have expansionist aims. As the scheme developed, lists of available housing were drawn up that suggested there would be room for no fewer than 4.8 million people.

Then, in the summer of 1939, the government began to spread the word about its plans. A leaflet issued by the Lord Privy Seal's office in July 1939 sought to explain what would be happening, how and why. "Read this and keep it carefully," warned the leaflet. "You may need it."

It went on: "We must see to it … that the enemy does not secure his chief objects – the creation of anything like panic, or the crippling dislocation of our civil life.

"The government have accordingly made plans for the removal from what

are called 'evacuable' areas to safer places called 'reception' areas, of school children, children below school age if accompanied by their mothers or other responsible persons, and expectant mothers and blind persons."

The scheme was a voluntary one, stressed the leaflet, but clearly the children would be safer and happier away from the big cities where the dangers would be greatest. When told to do so, schoolchildren would assemble at their schools and travel, with their teachers or other carers, by train. It would not be possible to let all parents know in advance where each child was to be sent, but they would be notified as soon as the movement was over. Children under five would have to be accompanied by their mothers or another responsible person, parents were told.

The leaflet finished by outlining the 'evacuable' areas: London including West Ham, East Ham, Walthamstow, Leyton, Ilford, Barking, Tottenham, Hornsey, Willesden, Acton and Edmonton; the Medway towns of Chatham, Gillingham and Rochester; Portsmouth, Gosport and Southampton in Hampshire; Birmingham and Smethwick in the Midlands; Liverpool,

Bootle, Birkenhead and Wallasey on Merseyside; the Lancashire industrial centres of Manchester and Salford; Sheffield, Leeds, Bradford and Hull on the other side of the Pennines; Newcastle and Gateshead in north-east England; and Edinburgh, Rosyth, Glasgow, Clydebank and Dundee in Scotland.

September 1 dawned to the extraordinary sight of multitudes of gas mask-equipped schoolchildren in those places, bearing address labels like pieces of luggage, being herded on to the trains that would take them to their new lives. Teachers' shouted instructions, sobbing and wailing children and mothers, impatient officials and snorting steam trains created chaotic scenes.

The government had recommended a list of clothing to be taken by the children on their travels: all were to have an overcoat, boots or shoes and plimsolls; boys should have one vest, one pair of pants, one pair of trousers, two pairs of socks, handkerchiefs and a pullover or jersey; girls should take one vest, one pair of knickers, one petticoat, two pairs of stockings, handkerchiefs, one slip, one blouse and one cardigan. In reality, many children were too poor to possess all the items on the list.

Far Left: Carrying gas masks and belongings, evacuees leave for safer homes.

CHILDREN
are safer in the country
. . . . leave them there

Yet for many evacuees, this seemed like an adventure or a holiday. Many had never experienced life outside their local areas, let alone in the countryside. Many years later, one evacuee from London recalled: "We marched to Waterloo station behind our head teacher, carrying a banner with our school's name on it. We all thought it was a holiday, but the only thing we couldn't work out was why the women and girls were crying."

Despite the initial chaos at the railway stations, the first three days of the evacuation seemed to work well. They certainly resulted in a radical redistribution of the population, with 1.5 million people finding themselves in new homes. This vast group was composed of 827,000 children of school age, 524,000 mothers with children under five, 13,000 pregnant women, 7,000 disabled people and more than

LEAVE THIS TO US SONNY — <u>YOU</u> OUGHT TO BE OUT OF LONDON

MINISTRY OF HEALTH EVACUATION SCHEME

100,000 teachers and others responsible for the children's care.

The *Daily Mirror* felt the evacuation had been so successful that it reported exuberantly: "Evacuation of schoolchildren from London went without a hitch. The children, smiling and cheerful, left their parents and entrained for unknown destinations in the spirit of going on a great adventure.

"'I wish all our passengers were as easy to manage', a railway official said. 'The children were very well behaved.'"

But behind the outwardly visible success of the scheme lay some uncomfortable realities. Many thousands of evacuees had been placed on the first available train, with the result that they had no idea where they were heading and many school and family groups were broken up. Further group break-ups came as the masses were herded off the

Above: Leave it to the experts, youngsters were told

mainline trains onto the smaller services that were to take them nearer to their new homes.

And, despite all the careful planning that had gone into the preparations for Operation Pied Piper, some reception areas were overwhelmed by sheer numbers of evacuees, while others found themselves welcoming people from different groups or social classes than the ones they had been expecting. Some evacuees had insufficient food to see them through the day. And, even more worrying, there didn't seem to be enough accommodation for the weary travellers.

What the government had failed to take into account when it carried out its survey of available housing was that some householders – generally the better off kind – would make their own arrangements for welcoming escapees from more vulnerable areas. Now, there was simply not enough bed space to go round.

What's more, many of the evacuees, deposited in places they had never dreamed existed, far from home, found themselves in rather unwelcoming atmospheres. Children were often simply lined up against a wall in the village hall while the prospective hosts inspected them before pronouncing: "I'll take that one." Some felt as if they were cattle being paraded in a market, and the humiliation and shame stayed with them for the rest of their lives.

Another method of finding host families entailed being taken from door to door in the town or village in the hope of finding a household that would take them in. The feeling of rejection as family after family turned away the young hopefuls can only be imagined.

There is also no getting away from

the fact that some children were also being exposed to new, sinister dangers. "It was little more than a paedophile's charter," says Steve Davis, a clinical psychologist who has specialised in trauma suffered in war.

It should be no surprise that many children did not take easily to their new lives. In addition to homesickness, some displayed more visible physical symptoms of their distress: some estimates of the number suffering from enuresis – better known as bedwetting – put the figure as high as 33 per cent. The Women's Voluntary Service was moved to publish a leaflet, *Bedwetting for householders taking unaccompanied children*, containing guidance on the problem.

There were other difficulties, of a social dimension. Many hosts had known little of the levels of poverty and deprivation endured by some urban families. Equally, some evacuees found it difficult to come to terms with the sleepy, more comfortable places they found themselves in, coming as they did from smoky, bustling urban areas. Some never adapted to their new surroundings, and bore lasting scars.

But happier memories of evacuation abound. One evacuee, Ivor Ball of Kent, remembers arriving at the home of his new 'foster mother'. "Little did I know that I was to spend some of the happiest days of my life in my short stay in her home," he told local historians.

The first morning of his new life must have seemed like a scene from an idyll. "I awoke the next morning and looked out of the window to a very peaceful scene. The river Wye was drifting silently by, glistening in the sunshine, a slight mist lifting from its waters. I had never really seen a river like this before, and I was impressed by the tranquillity of it all. The

scene was in complete contrast to the urgency of the days before, when we left Folkestone to the sound of heavy gunfire across the Channel."

Martin Vandervelde, from East Ham in east London, was another evacuee who found a welcome in the countryside. "The Izzards [their hosts in a village near Swindon] had no children of their own,

which was a great disappointment to them," he remembers. "So it was like a miracle to have two boys given to them for the duration of the war.

"We were taken home to their council house, eagerly fed and bathed in a copper bathtub with hot water from the kettle. When we went to bed we saw from the window that they had chickens

Nicht anfassen

Above: V-1 flying bombs, otherwise known as Doodlebugs, threatened Britain in the later stages of the war

in a pen in the back garden. This was a real novelty for us and it was promised that we could collect the eggs the next day. Suddenly I realised that living in the country was going to be a whole new experience. I had never seen chickens running around!"

Other evacuation stories were not quite so happy. Sonya Brett remembers when she was evacuated from Clapton in east London to a village in Cornwall. She and her sister were 'billeted' with a lady who, it seemed, had taken them just to get her hands on the government money available to hosts.

"We had to eat the food put in front of us and this proved a problem," Sonya recalls. "As we were Jewish, we knew we should not eat pork – and in fact, I could not eat it. I also remember that I could not understand the Cornish accent. I had great difficulty in understanding our foster mother and I was also very homesick.

"After about six weeks we were both ill – we both had thrush in our mouths and we also had lice in our hair. I had thick black curls and every time a flea was seen in my hair, my foster mother cut off another curl."

After three or four weeks, says Sonya, her mother travelled to Cornwall to see what was happening. "She said afterwards that she cried all night when she saw our condition. It took my mother a week to get our heads completely clean, and that was with washing every two or three hours. We then stayed with her on a neighbouring farm to recover."

Sonya's evacuation story ended happily, for she was eventually billeted with a far more satisfactory host family, and she was certainly not alone in being grateful for her wartime experiences. There are even stories of working class evacuees being treated as royalty, with servants to attend to their every need.

Talking to evacuees today often provokes memories of dreamlike rural existences living with hospitable foster parents and playing with kindly school friends, and of lives enriched by the experience. But you don't have to look far to find accounts of foster parents who were hostile, unfriendly, uncaring or even abusive.

David Prest, who made a series of programmes for BBC radio on the true story of wartime evacuation, recounts the grim tale of one evacuee from Bristol whose food rations were stolen by his host, who lived high on the hog while the child existed on a diet of mashed potatoes. He was eventually rescued, bruised and bleeding, by shocked police officers after being horsewhipped for speaking his mind. Then there was the case of another evacuee who, incredibly, was locked in a birdcage by his hosts, with no more than bread and water to eat.

Such shocking cases are, of course, unusual. Any worthwhile analysis of Operation Pied Piper must emphasise the enormity of the exercise and its relative success. And it must not be forgotten that it was not the only population evacuation experienced by Britain in World War II.

After the initial scattering of vulnerable groups to safer areas, many returned home once it became clear that the feared massive German bombing campaigns had yet to materialise. The so-called Phoney War ended abruptly in the summer of 1940, however, and new phases of evacuation began.

Between 13 and 18 June 1940, 100,000 children were evacuated – some of them for the second time – and efforts were made to clear vulnerable groups from coastal towns in the south-east of England and East Anglia. These were the areas that, with the fall of France, now faced the threat of German invasion. By July, more than 200,000 children had been evacuated.

Then came the Blitz – the sustained bombing campaign carried out by the Luftwaffe between September 1940 and May 1941. Here again was a sound reason for vulnerable people to leave the targeted areas, and free travel and billeting allowances were made available to children, the elderly, pregnant women, the disabled or sick and those who had lost their homes to German bombs. The population of London alone was eventually reduced by around a quarter, as some people able to make private arrangements for evacuation also took the opportunity to move.

Although aerial bombing remained a threat for the duration of the war, many evacuees gradually returned home to 'normal' life, and by the end of 1943 a mere 350,000 individuals were officially listed as billeted. By September 1944, despite the threat of V-1 flying bombs and V-2 rockets, it was felt conditions were safe enough for evacuation schemes to be brought to an end.

Evacuation changed Britain for ever. The eyes of evacuees were opened to new ways of life far removed from the stresses and strains of city living, and for some it was an experience that shaped their hopes and dreams for the rest of their lives. The eyes of some host families were equally opened to levels of urban poverty and squalor that had previously been hidden from them. The evacuation experience was a major contributory factor in the post-war blurring of dividing lines between social classes, the like of which Britain had never previously experienced.

Centre: Evacuees return home. By the end of 1943 just 350,000 people were listed as billeted

Plunged into Darkness

"Put that light out!" Anyone who has watched a few episodes of the classic comedy *Dad's Army* on television will be familiar with the outraged yell of ARP warden William Hodges, played by Bill Pertwee. It was also an order familiar to anyone in the real world of wartime Britain who broke the strict blackout regulations.

Hodges, officious busybody though he was, was only doing his job. Britain's 1.4 million Air Raid Precautions wardens, all unpaid volunteers, were in the frontline when it came to ensuring that not a single chink of light emitted from the ground would help Luftwaffe bomber pilots to carry out their deadly missions.

It stood to reason that the pilots' task of aiming their bombs accurately at their targets would be made more difficult if they had no lights to guide them. In addition, the otherwise reasonably simple job of navigating to and from targets would be more challenging in the absence of light.

In July 1939, two months before Britain's declaration of war on Germany, wardens were advised that it would take a high degree of discipline to ensure the blackout regulations were strictly enforced. And it didn't take long for those regulations to come into force. On 1 September – the same day that thousands took to the nation's railway network in the first mass wave

Left: Just doing his job – ARP warden Hodges finds himself the centre of attention in an episode of *Dad's Army*

of evacuations – the Lord Privy Seal's office issued an official notice. It read: "A lighting order has been made under Defence Regulation No 24 and comes into operation at sunset tonight as a further measure of precaution.

"The effect of the order is that every night from sunset to sunrise, all lights inside the buildings must be obscured and lights outside buildings must be extinguished, subject to certain exceptions in the case of external lighting where it is essential for the conduct of work on vital national importance. Such lights must be adequately shaded."

This was not the first time Britain, at least in parts, had been plunged into darkness as a means of defence against an airborne threat. German Zeppelin airships were used to launch bombing raids during World War I and local blackouts, brought into effect whenever a raid was detected, had some success in reducing their effectiveness. However, once fighter aircraft were developed that could take on the relatively cumbersome airships in the air, the Zeppelin threat was effectively nullified and the lights could go on again.

Nevertheless, German bombing raids, by Zeppelins and other aircraft, had accounted for nearly 1,000 casualties on British soil before World War I was brought to an end in 1918.

Bombing raids during World War

LITTLE BOOK OF **BRITAIN AT WAR**   25

II would operate on a different scale, however. The Luftwaffe's bombers, operating at high altitudes, represented a massive threat and would bring death and destruction wherever they flew. If their crews could not tell when they were passing over built-up areas, however, they might be forced to fly at lower altitudes, making them more vulnerable to ground-based air defence weapons and the fighter aircraft of the RAF.

Widespread trials of the effectiveness of blackout were carried out in the years leading up to the war, with some thought being given to partial restrictions on lighting. But by the time war became a reality, it had been decided that blackout would be total – except where the Air Ministry decided it would be beneficial to deceive Luftwaffe pilots, as we shall see later.

So in September 1939 the people of Britain set about ensuring their houses, places of work and leisure, shops, pubs and means of transport were compliant with the new regulations. And that entailed a great deal of work.

All windows and doors had to be covered by thick black curtains, cardboard or blackout paint, and the government made sure the necessary materials were available – although it also charged for them. If you were the proud owner of a large house, you found yourself facing a hefty bill, but it seems some leniency was shown towards members of the clergy forced to black out their vicarages.

Then there was the little matter of installing curtains. Householders often found that one thickness of fabric did not do the trick of stopping the light, so were forced to fold it once or even twice before the ARP warden was satisfied. Families whose windows had wooden frames were the lucky ones, for it was relatively easy for them to pin and unpin the fabric. Those who had metal or masonry frames faced a trickier installation.

Eventually, many families opted to pin black paper to the inside of their windows, but this solution was all too often a temporary one as paper put up and taken down tended not to last long, and numerous pinholes must have given window frames the appearance of being

Above: Only moonlight illuminates a street during the blackout

infested by woodworm.

Shopkeepers trading during the hours of darkness faced a particular problem: how to let customers in and out of their premises without any light escaping. This they often did by installing double doors, with one door being closed before the other was opened.

For the owners of factories with large expanses of glass roofing, the problems in complying with the regulations were challenging in the extreme. It proved impossible to cover up sources of light with temporary panels, and painting the glass black merely cut out natural light when it was needed in the daytime. Working day and night under artificial lighting proved unpopular and unhealthy for workers, and expensive for employers.

Streetlights and any other external sources of illumination were either switched off completely or dimmed and adapted so that the light shone downwards.

What about those people who needed to travel during the hours of blackout? All public transport vehicles – trains, buses, trams – were of course affected by the regulations, and private car drivers faced the same problem on a smaller scale. No interior lights were to be displayed and, at first, only sidelights were permitted to light the way forward. Later, the regulations were changed, for reasons we shall come to, to allow headlights to be used provided they were fitted with slotted covers so that their light was deflected towards the ground.

Cyclists were no exception to the rule; the upper halves of their lamps had to be completely obscured while the lower halves of reflectors were treated with black paint 'or otherwise rendered non-effective'.

Even pedestrians were affected by the regulations. If you were caught smoking in the street, with your cigarette emitting its telltale red glow, you could find yourself in court, and the story is told of a man who was prosecuted after striking a match in order to look for his false teeth. The court showed little leniency and he was fined 10 shillings. We do not know if he ever found his teeth.

The government also provided a welter of safety advice for pedestrians, communicated through posters and advertisements. Wear or carry something white when you're out, people were urged, and if you must walk on the road, always face the oncoming traffic. Men were even advised to leave their shirt tails hanging out so they could be seen by motorists. Luminous armbands were made available, and one poster went so far as to claim: 'Carrots keep you healthy and help you to see in the blackout'.

All these rules and regulations, and the enforcement of them, had drastic effects, some for the better and some for the worse. Many Britons found that the blackout helped to engender a remarkable community spirit, as everyone did their bit to divert the Luftwaffe's attentions, and many helped the ARP wardens by pointing out infringements of the law.

But the blackout's effects were much more far-reaching than that. It has been noted by one observer that it "transformed conditions of life more thoroughly than any other single feature of the war."

Far Left: An ARP warden informs the public of the official blackout time

Family life was certainly radically changed. As the historian Angus Calder observed in his book *The People's War*: "In the first place, most people had to spend five minutes or more every evening blacking out their homes. If they left a chink visible from the streets, an impertinent air raid warden or policeman would be knocking at their door, or ringing the bell with its new touch of luminous paint. There was an understandable tendency to neglect skylights and back windows.

"Having struggled with drawing pins and thick paper, or with heavy black curtains, citizens might contemplate going out after supper – and then reject the idea and settle down for a long read and an early night."

The blackout also brought to the attention of the law many people to whom the idea of being fined or appearing in court had previously been unthinkable. The regulations were strictly enforced – as they had to be – and the penalties could be severe. ARP wardens could fine transgressors, who would otherwise find themselves up in front of the magistrates. It has been calculated that nearly a million Britons had fallen foul of the blackout regulations by the end of the war, and many, many more must have been cautioned by generous ARP wardens.

Even a sociable night out at the pictures could have an unwanted ending. One 'victim' from Shropshire, who found an ingenious – but insufficient – use for his mother's underwear, told the BBC's researchers for *People's War*: "We used to go to Craven Arms cinema on Sunday nights. A gang of us went on pushbikes. We had to have red back lights. I broke the glass in mine and I couldn't find any red material to cover it. Instead, I used some pink material from a pair of my mother's knickers."

The intrepid film-lover said that when he came out of the cinema with his friend, she found that her light had been stolen. Undeterred, and needing to get home, they passed a sentry box as they were cycling out of the town. And out of the sentry box stepped a policeman.

"He took our names and addresses because my friend had no light and mine was pink instead of red. Next week we

Switch off that LIGHT!

LESS LIGHT – MORE PLANES

had a summons to go to court, but we wrote a letter and pleaded guilty. So we were fined five shillings each, which was about a week's wages for me."

Cries of "put that light out!" could sometimes be the cause of hilarity rather than hardship, though. One Liverpudlian told the BBC's researchers of the night an ARP warden hammered on his family's front door. "My dad went to the door and protested that we were not showing any lights," he continued.

"There followed a heated argument, until the warden said: 'Come across the road and see for yourself.' From across the street, a bright light showed in a bedroom window but, as my father pointed out, it was a reflection of the full moon." Exit, one assumes, one over-enthusiastic and rather sheepish warden.

Some effects of the blackout were more distressing than appearances in court. While darkening the streets might have made the people of Britain feel more sheltered from the attentions of German bombers, they were in fact much more at risk from other kinds of danger.

It hardly needs stating that getting about – whether on foot or in a vehicle – became many times more perilous in the absence of light. Driving a car became almost unimaginably difficult in the pitch dark; there was little chance of being able to see signposts, let alone other vehicles or pedestrians. As a result, the number of casualties on the roads rocketed. Just one statistic is enough to illustrate this fact: in September 1939, the number of people killed in road accidents rose by nearly 100 per cent.

The king's surgeon, Wilfred Trotter was later moved to write in the *British Medical Journal*: "By frightening the nation into blackout regulations, the Luftwaffe was able to kill 600 British citizens a month without ever taking to the air, at a cost to itself of exactly nothing."

Accidents were not confined to those caused by motor vehicles, of course. On the railways, passengers had enormous difficulty in making out where they were, as stations as well as trains were blacked out. How could you tell if you were at your destination if you couldn't see the signs on the platform? Even worse, if you couldn't see a thing outside, how could you tell you were at a station at all when the train stopped?

The *Daily Sketch* newspaper reported one unfortunate case in which a passenger, believing he had arrived at his station when the train had in fact stopped at a signal on a viaduct, stepped from the carriage and fell 80 feet. Miraculously, he survived, but many didn't live to tell the tale of similar accidents.

Pedestrians also faced enormous problems. Countless thousands of accidents were caused by the difficulty of walking down a street when you simply couldn't see the hand in front of your face. Injuries sustained from collisions with buildings or unlit lamp-posts, or from losing your footing as you stepped off an unseen kerb, ranged from broken noses to more serious fractures and even death.

The results of a survey published in January 1940 served to bring home the severity of the situation: by that stage, just four months after the introduction of the blackout, about one person in five could claim to have sustained some kind of injury because of it.

Then there was the problem of getting lost. A County Durham man told BBC researchers that, after stumbling around in utter darkness while out carol singing as an 11-year-old in 1940, he waited for a moonlit night before venturing out again. After a more successful evening he set off home, but his progress was

Far Left: Government posters reinforced the blackout message and helped to conserve energy

halted when he stumbled on a kerbstone and fell full length into the road. After recovering his composure he stumbled a few paces before realising he didn't know which direction he was heading.

He knew there were houses nearby but, too timid to try to find one and knock on the door, he staggered on "like a blind person with no assistance". Wooden fences surrounded the houses of his council estate, he realised, and he proceeded cautiously until he could feel the rough wood of the fencing. Now, by keeping the fence in his hands, he could make his way to the edge of the estate. It was with enormous relief that he heard the sound of a bus and realised he was approaching the main road through his village. Now in a familiar area, he was able to complete his journey home.

Complete darkness brought with it yet another problem: the fear of crime. Burglars, pickpockets and other thieves would find their profession much easier, it was thought, and there were great concerns about the vulnerability of women to the attentions of predatory men.

Despite the fears, there is little evidence to show that the enforced darkness brought about a big rise in overall crime, although there was a marked increase in the number of crimes committed by juveniles, much of which can be attributed to the blackout. And when it comes to sexual offences against women, the statistics tell a quite disturbing story.

The number of reported rapes in Britain was steady around the 100 per annum mark in the late 1930s, but it rose in 1940 to 125 and went on rising, to peak at 416 in 1944. The figures for indecent assault tell a similar story. It seems the blackout was capable of covering a multitude of sins.

In the face of all these problems stemming from the blackout, and with practical experience of its enforcement under its belt, the government acted at various times to soften the regulations. On motor cars, for example, it allowed dipped headlights, with the proviso that they should be covered by hoods with three slots, as we have seen.

To make life easier for pedestrians and drivers, many kerbstones were painted white, and white lines were added in the middle of roads. In a bid to reduce the number and seriousness of road casualties, the government also introduced a 20mph speed limit during the hours of darkness. It's said the first person to be convicted of speeding under this law was a hearse driver but that tale is, perhaps, apocryphal.

There were other ways to ease the problems of the blackout. Churches and market stalls could be partly lit, it was decided, and a later concession allowed illuminated signs at restaurants and cinemas. Local authorities were permitted to introduce 'glimmer' lighting – street-lamps emitting a little light in town centres and at road junctions.

Pedestrians were allowed to carry torches, although their beams had to be covered with tissue paper and directed downwards. The Ministry of Information offered guidance for those who were waiting for a bus: "Shine your torch in a downwards direction so that the beam lights up your feet. As the bus approaches, switch the light of the torch on and off twice."

At last, light could be glimpsed at the end of the tunnel, as well as in the streets. By September 1994, the German war machine's capability was diminished and the threat of aerial bombardment likewise reduced. It was announced that the people of Britain could now enjoy the relative luxury of a 'dim-out' at night – lighting with the equivalent of moonlight. The blackout could still be imposed in the event of an air raid alert, however.

The nation rejoiced heartily when full street lighting was restored in April 1945, and the lighting up of Big Ben in London came on 30 April. That symbolic illumination came five years and 123 days after the imposition of blackout.

A footnote to the story of the wartime blackout shows British ingenuity at its best. The plunging into darkness of the country's villages, towns, cities and other military targets provided the opportunity to practise a little deception on the enemy.

If Luftwaffe pilots could not make out their intended targets through the pitch dark, why not try to lure them, with a little judicious lighting, to false targets where their bombs would do no significant damage, or where they could be enveloped by anti-aircraft fire?

It worked, too. Many a German bomber navigator was attracted to a merrily burning fire or a deliberately illuminated 'town', far away from where he could do any damage.

Dodging Death from Above

Far Right:
Adolf Hitler – his
intention after 4
September 1940
was to eradicate
Britain's cities

Thousands of Nazi party members and sympathisers at the Berlin Sports Palace listened intently as Führer Adolf Hitler uttered the words that would condemn the people of Britain to five years of fear.

Hitler, speaking on 4 September 1940, was recalling the first bombing by British forces of the German capital, an event that had taken place on 25 August and marked a significant turning point in the war. "This is a game at which two can play," he intoned.

"When the British Air Force drops 2,000 or 3,000 or 4,000 kilogrammes of bombs, then we will drop 150,000, 180,000, 230,000, 300,000, 400,000 kilogrammes on a single night. When they declare they will attack our cities in great measure, we will eradicate their cities.

"The hour will come when one of us will break – and it will not be National Socialist Germany!"

So began the Blitz, the savage assault by the Luftwaffe on British cities that lasted for nine months, ceasing only in May 1941. And so began the war-long German campaign of bomb and rocket attacks that accustomed millions of Britons to nightly trips to air raid shelters and contributed massively to the awful toll of 67,000 civilian casualties.

Until Hitler spoke those fateful words, the Luftwaffe had been forbidden to bomb civilian areas. Now the full

fury of the huge German air force was unleashed on London and on many other towns and cities. All through the day and night of 7 September 1940, London suffered appalling damage as Luftwaffe aircraft dropped more than a million kilogrammes of bombs on the capital. And that was just the start.

London was the primary target of the Blitz, but cities like Belfast, Birmingham, Bristol, Cardiff, Clydebank, Coventry, Hull, Liverpool, Manchester and Southampton were firmly in the sights of Hermann Göring, Hitler's trusty Luftwaffe commander-in-chief. And as the war went on, it became apparent that nowhere in the United Kingdom could truly be called safe.

Hitler's avowed aim in bombing Britain was to terrorise the people, to bend and twist their morale to breaking point so that, when the inevitable German invasion could finally take place, his victorious ground troops would find a population already crushed, cowed and defeated, ready to bow to their new Nazi masters. But his thinking was to be proved absurdly over-optimistic.

Far from breaking the British people, the bombing brought them together and strengthened their determination to outlast the aggressor. The oft-quoted spirit of the Blitz prevailed and the people worked together to combat the enemy in a way Hitler could never have envisaged. Britons often came to regard the nightly trip to the air raid shelter as something of a nuisance rather than an occasion for terror.

There was fear in every heart, of course there was. But throughout the war, the Bulldog Breed rolled up their sleeves and got on with the job in hand.

As we saw in the last chapter, patrolling the front line of resistance to the Luftwaffe's attacks were the men and women wardens of Air Raid Precautions (ARP). The organisation had been set up in 1924 as the realisation grew of the awful toll that air raids could exact in time of war.

ARP wardens were given the task of distributing gas masks (38 million of them) and prefabricated air raid shelters, as well as the upkeep of public shelters, ensuring the blackout regulations were respected, and recruiting volunteers for civil defence and the emergency services. Their duties did not end there, however.

In their distinctive overalls, adorned by an ARP armlet, and their steel helmets (white for chief wardens, black for others), wardens were out in the streets during air raids, helping to deal with fires, administering first aid, manning ambulances, searching for casualties and helping to rescue those who had survived and search for those who hadn't.

Throughout the war, more than 1.4 million ARP wardens served the cause and, unlike warden Hodges in *Dad's Army*, they were seldom figures of fun, although a certain sense of humour was essential. Many were decorated for their sterling work and valour, and wardens were often in the line of fire themselves.

One warden in the Manchester area remembers a Christmas celebration in 1940 when 17 people were gathered in a three-storey house, which had a brick shelter and a reinforced cellar. The celebrations were interrupted as the air raid sirens sounded and the building was pulverised by a direct bomb hit. Eleven people in the building and a family of five next door were killed.

Completely buried and losing consciousness, the warden nevertheless managed to stick some fingers out of the rubble, and he was spotted by a soldier and dug out. Taken to hospital, he was left on the floor before being treated because of the sheer number of casualties. Afterwards, he spent three months convalescing.

But his story does not end there. On his first night back on duty he raced towards his ARP post as the sirens sounded once again, and witnessed another direct hit, this time on petrol storage tanks beside the Manchester Ship Canal. As he rushed to the scene yet another bomb burst and he was flung down a stairwell.

Our warden's reputation for being at the centre of trouble was growing, and his colleagues, believing he was jinxed, told him jokingly to go home and stay there. But he stayed on at the scene and, as the need for ambulance drivers arose,

Far Left:
Herman Göring – the Luftwaffe commander had major cities in his sights

he was volunteered on the grounds that he seemed to be indestructible.

A very few ARP wardens were paid, but by far the majority of them volunteered their services freely, and they were not the only ones who gave up their time – and sometimes their lives – to aid their nation when the enemy struck from the air.

There were the volunteers of the Royal Observer Corps, who were trained to detect, track, identify and report enemy aircraft; the fire watchers, whose job it was to look out for incendiary bombs and extinguish them before they could take hold; the Auxiliary Ambulance Service and the Auxiliary Fire Service (later the National Fire Service); and many others.

All of these men and women were no strangers to the grim scenes of injury, mutilation and death that so often accompanied air raids. But the level of casualties in Britain during World War II was cut drastically by the steps the government took to ensure citizens could take shelter from the bombs.

Many families, unable or unwilling to take refuge in public air raid shelters or the many underground places that were available, such as London Underground stations, built their own shelters. The author of this book has one such small, brick-built example in his back garden, still perfectly intact and dry all these years after the war, and now forming the foundation of a flourishing rockery. Other families huddled in cellars or under the stairs. But many thousands of others took advantage of the offer of the curious construction that was known as the Anderson Shelter.

Designed in 1938 at the request of the Home Office, these curved, galvanised corrugated steel shelters were named after the Lord Privy Seal, Sir John Anderson, and were designed to take six people. They were distributed free to families with an income below £250 a year, but they could also be bought for £7 by those on higher incomes. And they were popular: 1.5 million were issued before the start of the war, and by the end of the conflict that number had risen to 3.6 million.

Six feet high, four feet six inches wide and six feet six inches long, Anderson Shelters were designed to be buried four feet in the ground and covered by at least 15 inches of soil. Some families used the soil to grow flowers or vegetables,

Far Left: The Luftwaffe's bombing campaigns did little to break the spirit of the British people

and shelter owners often organised competitions that recognised the best-planted shelter in the neighbourhood.

They may have looked rickety and a bit on the amateurish side, but Anderson Shelters did the job they were designed to do – withstand a bomb blast – reasonably well. What they didn't do, to the dismay of their occupants, was keep humans warm or keep water out, especially on cold, rainy winter nights.

One east London resident who was a child during the war has mixed memories of her family's Anderson Shelter. "Dad painted it and it had bunk beds on both sides, allowing four people to sleep in it," she remembers. "Just as Dad had finished painting it and put a small amount of furniture in it, workmen came and cemented the floor. Dad was not amused!

"There was no ventilation; only a small amount came through cracks in the door. It was always damp and had condensation running down the walls. There were also many spiders and other wrigglies."

Perhaps some kind of shelter erected inside the family home would do the trick, mused the authorities. So

the Morrison Shelter – official name: Table (Morrison) Indoor Shelter – came into being.

This one was named after the Home Security Minister, Herbert Morrison, and could be claimed free of charge by households with incomes lower than £350 a year. Half a million self-assembly kits had been distributed by the end of 1941, with another 100,000 being taken up in 1943 as the threat of the doodlebug flying bomb loomed.

Owners of a Morrison Shelter, once they had bolted the 359 parts together with the three tools provided, were faced with a construction six feet six inches long, four feet wide and two feet six inches high. It had steel plate an eighth of an inch thick on top, wire mesh sides and a metal lath floor, and its ingenious design sheltered its occupants from a falling floor in the event of their house collapsing. What's more, it could be used as a dining table during the day.

"The Morrison Shelter was warm because it was designed like an enormous bed with a lid," recalls a Middlesex resident. "Family members who were still at home during the Blitz, plus whoever happened to be visiting when the air raid siren sounded, would simply pile in. The body count would generally amount to three adults, three children and one dog."

The Morrison Shelter, like the Anderson, did a remarkable job. One research study found that, in 44 severely damaged houses accommodating 136 people where it had been installed, no fewer than 120 had escaped serious injury. A mere three people had been killed and 13 seriously injured.

Home-based shelters were not for everyone, however. How could you have an Anderson Shelter if you had no garden, or a Morrison if interior space was too limited? Not everyone had a basement or cellar, and simple trenches had obvious shortcomings. So spaces of a more public nature played an enormous role in sheltering the British people from Hitler's fury.

The range of places in which one could take refuge was enormous: some towns and cities had networks of underground tunnels or caves; railway arches could keep dozens safe; underpasses beneath roads and railways were fairly popular; but much post-war attention has focused on the use of

London's Underground stations as air-raid shelters.

Despite the fact that they had been used with success in World War I, the use of Tube stations and other deep shelters was not a popular option among the authorities in the early days of the war. Many negative factors were quoted, including the lack of toilet facilities, the potential for spreading diseases, the danger of people falling onto electrified lines and the fear that folk would be tempted to stay in the stations day and night. But the government was forced to bow to people pressure.

On 19 September 1940, countless Londoners, some equipped with bedding, most carrying food rations, took matters into their own hands and started occupying Tube station platforms as early as 4pm. And there they stayed until the following morning. Metropolitan Police officers did nothing to deter them and in many cases they were helped out by sympathetic station managers, who ensured the crowds had access to adequate toilet facilities.

The government was not slow to realise that a ban on the use of Tube stations would now be fruitless and might result in more civil disobedience,

DODGING DEATH FROM ABOVE

and in a remarkable about-turn set about organising things properly. Whole sections of track were closed to trains and concreted over; 79 stations were equipped with bunks that could accommodate 22,000 people; 'marshals' were appointed to help shelterers and maintain order; chemical toilets were installed; first aid facilities were provided; canteens were set up to serve food and drink. In addition, eight deep-level shelters were built underneath Tube stations during the war.

In truth, it was what should have happened in the first place. It's thought that 170,000 people regularly took advantage of the shelter provided by the Tube stations during the war, and many of them escaped the injury or death that might otherwise have befallen them.

On the negative side, Londoners sheltering in the Tube had to endure what must have been a thoroughly unpleasant experience. The degree of comfort was not high, making sleep difficult if not impossible; families were inclined to jealously guard 'their' space, and it was not unknown for disputes to boil over into fights; and the stench of so many bodies crammed into a relatively airless space for so many hours must have been overpowering.

And these shelters were not completely safe from bombs, either; some of the Luftwaffe's high-explosive bombs were capable of penetrating 50 feet through solid ground, and there could be fatalities when bombs scored direct hits on or around the Tube stations, especially where a station was set fairly shallowly in the ground. But the worst catastrophe of the war occurred not as a result of German bombs but through human frailty.

On the evening of 3 March 1943, sirens alerted the people of an area of east London to the likelihood of an air raid, and hundreds set off at a run to Bethnal Green Tube station. From homes, cinemas and buses they converged on the station, which was fitted with 5,000 bunks and could take in 10,000 altogether. Up to 600 people had already taken their places on the platforms when the alert sounded.

It must be said that this particular station was not ideally equipped to handle sudden influxes of large numbers of people, despite the large number it could accommodate. It had just one narrow entrance and no crush barriers, and its first staircase was dimly lit by a single 25 watt bulb. Nevertheless, 1,500 people had entered by 8.27pm, when a terrifying sound split the night air.

Londoners were used to the sounds of falling and exploding bombs, but this was something new and entirely different. A newly installed anti-aircraft rocket battery nearby fired a salvo of 60 rockets with a terrific roar and the crowd at the shelter entrance, in panic, surged forward. Near the bottom of the first staircase, a woman fell. A man tripped over her, others followed and within seconds hundreds of fallen people were jamming the staircase.

With a huge crush of people doing their best to escape the terror and push into the station, rescue proved impossible until it was too late. An appalling total of 173 people suffocated to death.

News of the tragedy was suppressed until after the war, the government fearing that its publication would cause wider panic among the populace.

There were further alternatives to the air raid shelters we have already discussed. Street communal shelters, for example, were built to cater for people caught in the streets when the sirens sounded, car drivers and passengers and

OFFICIAL INSTRUCTIONS ISSUED BY THE MINISTRY OF HOME SECURITY

GAS ATTACK

HOW TO PUT ON YOUR GAS MASK

Always keep your gas mask with you – day and night. Learn to put it on quickly. Practise wearing it.

1. Hold your breath. 2. Hold mask in front of face, with thumbs inside straps.
3. Thrust chin well forward into mask, pull straps over head as far as they will go.
4. Run finger round face-piece taking care head-straps are not twisted.

IF THE GAS RATTLES SOUND

1. Hold your breath. Put on mask wherever you are. Close window.

2. If out of doors, take off hat, put on your mask. Turn up collar.

3. Put on gloves or keep hands in pockets. Take cover in nearest building.

IF YOU GET GASSED

 BY VAPOUR GAS Keep your gas mask on even if you feel discomfort. If discomfort continues go to First Aid Post

BY LIQUID or BLISTER GAS

1	2	3	4
Dab, but *don't rub* the splash with handkerchief. Then destroy handkerchief.	Rub No. 2 Ointment well into place. *(Buy a 6d. jar now from any chemist). In emergency chemists supply Bleach Cream free.*	If you can't get Ointment or Cream within 5 minutes wash place with soap and warm water	Take off at once any garment splashed with gas.

PRINTED FOR H.M. STATIONERY OFFICE BY FOSH & CROSS LTD., LONDON. 151/504c

pedestrians among them.

With materials supplied by the government and erected by local builders from March 1940 onwards, these shelters boasted 14 inch-thick brick walls and one foot-thick reinforced concrete roofs. They were designed to accommodate in the region of 50 people at a time and were divided into sections, with each section containing six bunks.

But street communal shelters were not popular with their users. Rumours of accidents – such as the one about a shelter being filled with water when a main burst, drowning its occupants – began to spread, and the rumours were sometimes founded in reality. Deaths certainly did occur when shelters' walls were shaken by bomb blasts, with the result that the concrete roofs fell in on those seeking shelter.

When stocks of bricks and concrete began to run low, the days of the communal street shelter were numbered, and Britons sought out other solutions to their air raid shelter needs.

Besides the Luftwaffe's increasingly sophisticated bombs, another fear haunted the people of Britain throughout World War II: gas.

The Great War of 1914-18 – when use of poison gases like chlorine, mustard gas and phosgene had been fairly common on the battleground – was still fresh in many people's minds. Many dreadfully crippled ex-servicemen were a regular reminder of the terrors of gas. Too many Britons had seen the awful effects of gas attacks, and were perhaps familiar with Wilfred Owen's lines written from the WWI front line:

Gas! GAS! Quick, boys! – An ecstasy of fumbling
Fitting the clumsy helmets just in time,
But someone still was yelling out and stumbling
And flound'ring like a man in fire or lime.
–
Dim through the misty panes and thick green light,
As under a green sea, I saw him drowning.

The Germans had used gas in World War I (as had the British, incidentally), went the argument, so why would they hesitate to use it on a civilian population this time round? More effective gases, even nerve agents like sarin and soman, which could be delivered from ships, aircraft and rockets, were in production and available.

The British government was concerned enough about this threat to ensure that just about everybody in the country – a total of 38 million people – had been issued with a gas mask, and the instructions on how to use them, by September 1939. The population was also told to carry a gas mask at all times in case of an attack.

It is no exaggeration to say that gas masks were detested, although they were a constant source of black humour. Adults' versions resembled nothing so much as a pig's snout, while those for children were nicknamed Mickey Mouse or Donald Duck. And there were also awful contraptions designed for babies. It was difficult to breathe while wearing a mask, which smelt overpoweringly of rubber and disinfectant.

Constant reminders in newspaper advertisements and on posters nagged away at the people: always carry your gas mask. And in case people with dentures were unsure whether they should have their false teeth in or out while donning a mask, one ad sternly advised: "Yes! If you don't, your mask may not fit properly, and a perfect fit is essential."

Britain got used to the masks and the cardboard boxes in which they were carried, although many were left, accidentally on purpose perhaps, on public transport and many a box was used to store other useful items. But in the event, they were never needed.

Gas attack was one danger British civilians never had to face.

Centre: Public street shelters were a common sight in wartime Britain

51

Waste Not, Want Not

The chances are that when a younger person asks someone who lived on the British home front during World War II about their experiences, the subject of rationing will crop up fairly rapidly. "Of course, we had very little tea or sugar in those days," the reminiscence will go, "and bananas were as rare as hen's teeth."

They were indeed, as were many other kinds of fruit. To get your hands on an orange you generally had to be very lucky and either pregnant or a needy youngster, unless you knew an extra-generous and resourceful greengrocer. Even everyday items like butter, milk and tea were in short supply and their distribution was strictly controlled.

DEFENC

BREACHES (

The undermention

Court	Date
HENDON - -	29th Aug., 191
WEST HAM -	29th Aug., 191
SMETHWICK -	22nd July, 191
OLD STREET -	4th Sept., 191
OLD STREET -	4th Sept., 191
CHESTER-LE-STREET	4th Sept., 191
HIGH WYCOMBE	7th Sept., 191

And foodstuffs were not the only subjects of rationing: also on the list were petrol, clothing, furniture, cosmetics and other commodities. The impact of rationing was hard and long lasting, and it was felt by everyone.

OF THE REALM. E.P. 6.

STRY OF FOOD.

THE RATIONING ORDER

victions have been recently obtained:—

Nature of Offence	Result
fully obtaining and using ration books -	3 Months' Imprisonment
a retailer & failing to detach proper number of coupons	Fined £20
ning meat in excess quantities - - -	Fined £50 & £5 5s. costs
a retailer selling to unregistered customer	Fined £72 & £5 5s. costs
etaching sufficient coupons for meat sold -	Fined £25 & £2 2s. costs
a retailer returning number of registered customers in excess of counterfoils deposited - - - -	Fined £50 & £3 3s. costs
false statement on application for and using Ration Books unlawfully - - - - - - - -	Fined £40 & £6 4s. costs

Enforcement Branch, Local Authorities Division,

The introduction of rationing early in the war came as no great surprise. It had been experienced towards the end of World War I, when German U-boats were achieving great success in sinking merchant ships that were carrying supplies and food to Britain. The government had even made preparations for rationing in the run-up to the General Strike of 1926, although as it turned out no such measures were needed.

At the beginning of September 1939,

a phrase more familiar nowadays than 70 years ago, the introduction of rationing was a no-brainer.

And it started with the control of petrol and diesel for motor vehicles, for the armed forces' need for oil-based fuels greatly outweighed that of any civilian. Meanwhile, the Ministry of Food was busy printing and issuing ration books to every man, woman and child in Britain, and advising them to register at their local shops.

But food rationing did not begin officially until 8 January 1940, when sugar, bacon and butter were declared subject to the regulations. They were followed by cheese, meat, eggs, milk, lard, tea, biscuits, jam, breakfast cereals and canned fruit, and queues were soon forming outside local shops throughout the country. Housewives bearing shopping baskets and ration books were determined to ensure their families got what they were entitled to – and to make sure no one else got anything extra.

The system was simple enough. Everyone had a ration book full of coupons, each of which could be cut out and used when buying the appropriate amount of foods. So every time a housewife wanted some butter,

as Britain declared war on Germany, the facts facing the country's planners were simple: the country produced less than a third of its food needs at home, and was heavily reliant on imports. In addition, German U-boats were once again patrolling the oceans, ready to target incoming merchant vessels with their precious cargoes of commodities like fruit, sugar, meat and cereals. To use

she would hand a butter coupon to the shopkeeper. If she discovered that she'd already used that week's coupon, she would get no butter that day.

How much was our housewife entitled to? Here's a typical example of one adult's weekly allowance:

Bacon and ham – 4oz
Butter – 2oz
Cheese – 2oz
Margarine – 4oz
Cooking fat – 4oz, sometimes 2oz
Milk – sometimes 3pts
Sugar – 8oz
Preserves – 1lb every two months
Tea – 2oz
Eggs – one shell egg a week if available
Dried eggs – one pack a month
Sweets – 12oz a month
Plus a monthly points scheme for fish, meat, fruit or peas

Meat was allocated according to price rather than weight, so cheaper cuts started to enjoy higher popularity than before. Rations varied according to what was available, but the above gives a good idea of the basic foodstuffs allocated to one individual.

To this could be added vegetables

Above: Rations tended to vary according to what was available.

(which were not rationed but were all too often in short supply), perhaps some home-grown fruit, and maybe some tinned goods, dried fruit, preserves, biscuits, cereals and pulses. Housewives often saved up their coupons, or pooled them with friends or neighbours, in order to make a little go a long way.

Certain other food categories were not subject to rationing, among

NH 3614995   NH 361499

Motor Fuel Ration Book

MOTOR CAR

1501 – 2200 C.C.

14 – 19 H.P.

Registered No. of Vehicle	Registered No of Vehic
Date and Office of Issue	Date and Office of Issue

This book is the property of Her Majesty's Government

Instructions to Issuing Cle

See that the issu of this Ratio Book is Recorde on the applicant' registration book

This portion, after com pletion, to be detache and forwarded to th Regional Petroleum Officer with Form P 221

The coupons in this book authorise the furnishing and acquisition of the number of units of motor fuel specified on the coupons.

them fish, yet it was often in short supply – hardly surprising given the dangers fishermen faced in putting to sea in U-boat-infested waters. Long queues were a common sight at fish and chip shops, where customers often complained about the appalling standard of the chips due to the low quality of oils available.

Other unrationed foods came on to the market towards the end of the war, including whale meat and a real curiosity – snoek, a fish that inhabits the waters around South Africa. Neither of these delicacies appealed much to the wartime Briton, it has to be said, and the popularity of whale meat can be gauged from the corruption of the lyric of a Vera Lynn song, sung ironically: "Whale meat again …"

Memories of the trials and tribulations of rationing are vivid. One Lancashire woman told researchers: "During the war the food situation was bad. [Her husband's] mother [with whom they were living] had 11 children and of course food was on ration. We used to have to eke everything out, and we maybe only got one pot of jam every four weeks or so.

"You had to stand in a queue for nearly everything. [Her husband's] mother used to stand in Jenkin's shop for cakes, but Grandma liked to bake bread. My own mother used to make sheep's head soup in the set pot when she was able to get a sheep's head off the butcher. The set pot was also used to wash all the clothes in, but everything was scrubbed out clean.

"Then she used to take jugs of this soup around to other neighbours and friends. All the people did that, sharing out whatever food there was."

A Sheffield woman, a housewife during the war, recalled: "Everyone was on the look-out for extras. You could sometimes pick up garden produce from friends, and occasionally local farmers would have sales, which provided potatoes, turnips, carrots and onions. You would get to know about these sales by word of mouth, and it would sometimes be a very long, tiring journey, carrying the heavy vegetables home – but it was worth it."

Those two reminiscences show to some extent how Britons relied on their own creativeness and resourcefulness, and that of others, to make up shortfalls in the rations, and to make what they had go that much further – even the dreaded dried egg powder. The Ministry of Food

Right: Rationing of motor fuel began before that of food, and continued after the war

Above: German U-boat attacks disrupted the flow of imports to Britain

Banana essence or extract
Sugar to taste

Method:

Choose young parsnips if possible, for they are more tender and have a sweeter taste. Peel the parsnips, do not slice.

Either cook in a small amount of unsalted water until tender or put into a steamer, cover and cook over boiling water. Dry the parsnips.

Slice the cooked parsnips and put into a bowl and mash. Add a few drops only of banana essence or extract. Continue adding flavouring until you get the right taste. Add sugar to taste, then mash until smooth. Use as a sandwich filling or as a pudding with custard.

Et voilà, in the absence of the real thing, Mock Banana! And there were plenty of other mock recipes doing the rounds during the war, including 'cream' (margarine, milk and cornflour) and 'goose' (lentils and breadcrumbs). Carrots sometimes replaced sugar in fruit tarts and, believe it or not, were sometimes eaten on sticks as impromptu lollies.

One popular recipe provided by

helped by producing posters, leaflets and cinema advertisements featuring tips for food use, and six million people tuned in every day to listen to Marguerite Patten's cooking advice programme on the wireless.

Patten could justifiably be called one of the first celebrity chefs (she later transferred to television), and her recipes were eagerly copied down and rustled up to feed many a family. One of them, designed to use only what might be available in the average store cupboard, was the Mock Banana:

Ingredients:

Parsnips

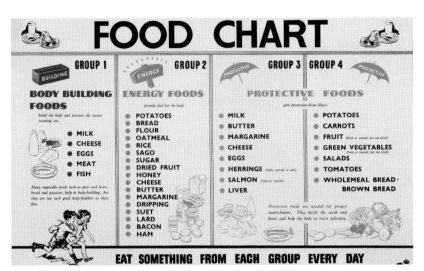

FOOD CHART

GROUP 1	GROUP 2	GROUP 3	GROUP 4

BODY BUILDING FOODS

build the body and prevent the tissues wearing out

- MILK
- CHEESE
- EGGS
- MEAT
- FISH

Many vegetable foods such as peas and beans, bread and potatoes, help in body-building; but they are not such good body-builders as these five.

ENERGY FOODS

provide fuel for the body

- POTATOES
- BREAD
- FLOUR
- OATMEAL
- RICE
- SAGO
- SUGAR
- DRIED FRUIT
- HONEY
- CHEESE
- BUTTER
- MARGARINE
- DRIPPING
- SUET
- LARD
- BACON
- HAM

PROTECTIVE FOODS

give protection from illness

- MILK
- BUTTER
- MARGARINE
- CHEESE
- EGGS
- HERRINGS *(fresh, canned or salt)*
- SALMON *(fresh or canned)*
- LIVER

- POTATOES
- CARROTS
- FRUIT *(fresh or canned, but not dried)*
- GREEN VEGETABLES *(fresh or canned, but not dried)*
- SALADS
- TOMATOES
- WHOLEMEAL BREAD · BROWN BREAD

Protective foods are needed for proper nourishment. They build the teeth and bones and help the body to resist infection.

EAT SOMETHING FROM EACH GROUP EVERY DAY

Left: The Ministry of Food issued advice on good nutrition

the government during the rationing years was Woolton's Vegetable Pie. Named after the minister for food, Lord Woolton, it was useful for cooks who had already used up the week's meat ration but had access to a supply of vegetables.

Ingredients:

2lb of potatoes
1lb of cauliflower
1lb of carrots
0.5lb of swede
0.5lb of parsnips
3 or 4 spring onions
Water for cooking
1 teaspoon of vegetable extract
1 tablespoon of oatmeal
Chopped parsley
2oz grated cheese.

Method:

Cook half the potatoes, the vegetables, the vegetable extract and oatmeal for 10 minutes in enough water to cover them. Stir occasionally to prevent sticking. Cool and place in a pie dish. Sprinkle with chopped

DIG FOR VICTORY

Despite the shortages and the frustrations of rationing, there is plenty of evidence to show that the population of Britain benefited from rationing. The average diet was certainly a lot healthier than its modern-day counterpart, obesity was likewise rare, and equal rations for all ensured the poorer members of society were better fed than they had been during the depression-hit years of the 1930s. In addition, the fact that so many people started growing their own fruit and vegetables in response to official pleas to Dig for Victory (which we'll examine in a later chapter) had a positive effect on the fitness of people living and working on the home front.

And the population, while perhaps hungry, could rejoice in the fact that by sacrificing a little food they were helping the war effort. Their contribution was recognised in a Ministry of Food poster that proclaimed:

parsley. Boil, then mash the rest of the potatoes; spread them over the vegetables to make a crust. Sprinkle the cheese on top.
Bake at 190C, 375F, gas mark 5 until lightly browned. Serve with gravy and vegetables. Serves six to eight.

Because of the pail, the scraps were saved.
Because of the scraps, the pigs were saved.
Because of the pigs, the rations were saved.
Because of the rations, the ships were saved.
Because of the ships, the island was saved.
Because of the island, the empire was saved.
And all because of the housewife's pail.

One way of supplementing the meagre food ration was, of course, to eat out – if you could afford it. At first, restaurants were exempted from the restrictions but this did not find favour among the general populace, for it meant the better-off could eat out often and well. As a result, regulations were introduced that meant no meal could cost more than five shillings, consist of more than three courses or contain both meat and fish.

Still, however, eating out in restaurants was not within the reach of many people, and it was partly in response to this that the establishments known as British Restaurants were set up.

The main aim behind British Restaurants, which used locations like church halls or schools, was to ensure that those who had run out of rationing coupons, or had perhaps been bombed out of their homes, would not go hungry. Established by the Ministry of Food and originally called Community Feeding Centres, they were run on a non profit-making basis by local authorities and offered meals for a maximum of 9d – equivalent to about £1 at today's prices. No meal contained more than

Go through your wardrobe

Make-do and Mend

one serving of meat, game, poultry, fish, eggs or cheese.

In smaller locations that did not qualify for one of these establishments, it was sometimes possible to set up a Cash and Carry Restaurant, from where meals delivered from a British Restaurant could be picked up.

Above: The ancient habit of making do and mending reached its peak during World War II

Above: Freelance entrepreneurs – otherwise known as spivs – like Private Walker in *Dad's Army* were often on hand to supplement rations

By the time the war was coming to an end there were around 2,000 British Restaurants in London alone, although it has to be said they were more popular in the capital than elsewhere. Popular or not, they were another example of ingenuity coming to the rescue in a time of need.

Here's a strange twist in the story of rationing in wartime Britain: when clothing rationing was introduced on 1 June 1941 no appropriate coupons had been distributed, so people were allowed to use any unused margarine coupons they had in their books in exchange for clothes.

It wasn't always quite so disorganised, however. As the scheme got going, it became clear that each person was allowed a total of 66 clothing coupons a year, which equated to one full outfit. Not many people on the home front built up extensive wardrobes during the war years, for as time went on the 66-point allowance was cut to 48, then 36 and finally 24 points.

Let's put the clothing ration into context. A man using up his 66 points would find he could buy an overcoat (18 coupons), a suit (up to 29), a pair of shoes (nine) and a pair of underpants (four) before his ration was exhausted. If he needed a shirt or two or some socks, it would be a case of patching up old garments until the following year.

To make matters worse for the dedicated follower of fashion, in 1942 regulations were introduced that sought to cut down on the amount of materials used in the manufacture of clothes. This meant that our hypothetical man using his 29 points to buy a suit would find it could have a maximum of three pockets and three buttons, trouser legs of 48cm maximum length and no turn-ups at all. On ladies' clothing there were to be no fancy belts and no elastic waistbands, and shoe heels were to be no higher than 5cm.

The centuries-old habit of making do and mending, of recycling old clothes and old materials, of improvising, reached its zenith during World War II. It was far from uncommon for women to use make-up to draw lines down the backs of their legs in imitation of stocking seams, and many an old curtain came back to life as a dress or skirt.

And foolish was the housewife who did not keep an eye open at all times for a bargain. One woman told researchers: "I remember my delight in coming across a dress which, the shop owner assured me, required no coupons at all – although this was reflected in the price. It was only when I got it home I realised it was made from dyed hessian."

The same woman recalled that the material used to make barrage balloons (large balloons tethered to the ground that were used to defend against low-level aircraft attack) made excellent waterproof raincoats, and silk parachutes, if they could be found, could be unpicked and restitched to make luxurious underwear. There was many a race between civilians and authorities to get to the landing point of an airman who had bailed out.

The reminiscence continues: "Worst of all was the shortage of accessories for clothing and the especially vital elastic was very difficult to obtain. What problems this caused; yet what ingenuity and inventiveness it inspired! Tape, string, cord or buttons and faith had to be relied upon to hold up garments. Nor was it any use depending upon a safety pin. These, too, were hard to come by, since all metal was needed for munitions."

The greatest humiliation, the woman recalled, came when the fastening on knickers suddenly gave way, but the resourceful girl soon learned to cope. She had three choices: step neatly out of the knickers and pocket them; leave them lying and walk on calmly, pretending they weren't hers; or clamp a hand in a vice-like grip on her waist, keeping it there until she reached a place of sanctuary.

Wherever and whenever a shortage of anything occurs, you will find men and women willing to bend or break the rules in order to satisfy the demand. This is when the black market opens for business.

For the less scrupulous Briton living through the privations of the rationing system, the friendly local spiv was always on hand to help out. This type of entrepreneur, dealing in black market or even more dodgy goods ("They fell off the back of a lorry, guv, as God's my witness"), came to be recognised by his expensive suit with padded shoulders, garish tie, pencil moustache and battered suitcase – a lot like Private Walker in *Dad's Army*, in fact. From the suitcase or from within his voluminous overcoat the spiv – sometimes known as the wide boy – would dispense watches, nylons, cosmetics; whatever was in demand and whatever he could lay his hands on, by fair means or foul.

And those goods weren't always what they were cracked up to be by the vendor. One woman remembered a friend buying a packet of tights that had supposedly come from America. "When she got home she found she had three 'pairs' with one leg on each," she reported.

Some spivs, far from being the lovable rogues they are often portrayed as, made fortunes from those affected by the misfortunes of war, but they weren't the only ones dabbling in the black market. It was far from unknown for shopkeepers to get in on the act. Goods could be sourced through frowned-upon channels and kept under the counter for favoured or wealthy customers, or a butcher might be persuaded to exceed a housewife's meat ration in exchange for half a dozen eggs – a lot like Corporal Jones in *Dad's Army*, in fact.

The authorities, naturally, took a dim view of the black market. One MP called this unofficial trade "treason of the very worst kind", and there were even calls for thrashings with the cat-o'-nine-tails for offenders. But the real penalties were severe enough. Laws passed during the war empowered the courts to impose prison sentences of up to two years, fines of up to £500 (an enormous sum in those days) plus three times the amount of money involved in the deal concerned.

No fewer than 900 inspectors were eventually working in Britain to combat the workings of the black market, and they found that the main source of food finding its way through the illegal channels were farmers and smallholders. But whatever the source and whatever the goods being traded, it proved impossible to stamp out the black market completely.

We have not touched on many of the goods that were rationed in wartime Britain. Besides food, clothing, oil-based fuels and furniture, they included soap, paper (newspapers were limited to 60 per cent of their pre-war usage) and coal. Even bread was rationed, although that didn't happen until after the war in 1946, when there was still an acute shortage of cereals. Rationing of many goods continued for several years after 1945.

Gradually supplies and the economy started to pick up, and bread was taken off the list in July 1948, followed by jam in December of that year, tea in 1952, sweets, cream, eggs and sugar in 1953 and meat, butter, margarine cheese and cooking fats in 1954.

Children who were born in the late 1950s or afterwards have little idea what their parents went through in order to put meat on the table during the dark days of the war.

Above: The material used in barrage balloons – here seen over London – could be used to make improvised raincoats

Women on the Home Front

Britain would not have been on the winning side in World War II without the enormous contribution of its women to the war effort. And that contribution did not just come from the 460,000 or so who were serving in the armed forces by the end of the war. From the millions of women who kept the wheels of industry turning to the 80,000 who laboured on farms in the Land Army, and from the ambulance drivers and firewatchers to the welfare workers of the Women's Voluntary Service, women's work was vital.

And it was revolutionary, too. When the war ended in May 1945, more than 6.5 million women were engaged in civilian war work, and a large proportion of them were working in roles that had previously been filled by men. In innumerable cases, women enjoyed and excelled at the work, even though they were paid less than men. The days of sharply delineated 'men's jobs' and 'women's work' were numbered.

Although they operated in non-combat roles, women serving in the auxiliary services of the army, navy and air force provided essential support to the men who were waging war on land, sea and air. Three months into hostilities, 39,000 women had volunteered for work in the auxiliary services including operating switchboards, cooking, cleaning, typing and driving, but many

found themselves in occupations of a more military nature. Motorcycle messengers were needed, as were women who could identify aircraft and plot the movements of aircraft and ships.

Members of the Auxiliary Territorial Service, the women's branch of the army, were known as ATS and were at first typically employed as cooks, storekeepers or clerks on home soil.

Soon, however, ATS were deployed to France, and some telephonists were among the last British personnel to leave the country at the fall of Dunkirk.

Some members of the First Aid Nursing Yeomanry (FANY), which operated in World War II as part of the ATS, also saw service overseas working for the Special Operations Executive, and were engaged in spying, sabotage and reconnaissance work behind enemy lines. Of 39 former FANY women sent by the SOE to France, 12 were captured and died in concentration camps. Among the agents were the distinguished figures of Violette Szabo, Odette Sansom and Noor Inayat Khan, who were all decorated for their courage and outstanding work.

In December 1941 the National Service Act made it compulsory for unmarried women between 20 and 30 to serve in one of the armed forces or choose to carry out civilian war work. Married women were also later called up and the age range extended from 19 to 43, and by June 1944, something like 450,000 women were serving in the auxiliary services.

One ATS was posted to Yorkshire as a wireless operator. She recalled: "We worked in shifts to cover 24 hours a day in a cycle of four days. The shifts lasted between seven and nine hours, during which we listened to and recorded transmissions, often through static and interference.

"The wireless station was in an isolated place out on the moors, and we tended to lose touch with the real world. It was hard work and living in

a barrack room for part of the time, especially in winter when it was bitterly cold, was not easy. We took turns to light the barrack room stove and the accepted method was to kick it and say: 'Light, you swine!'"

The roles available to members of the Women's Royal Naval Service – known as Wrens – included those of mechanic, weapons analyst, radar plotter, electrician and transport plane pilot. Slogans on recruitment posters urged: "Join the Wrens – free a man for the fleet".

Members of the Women's Auxiliary Air Force enjoyed a nickname too – they were called Waafs – and there were more than 180,000 of them at the service's peak in 1943. Waafs could work at weather forecasting, telephony and telegraphy, reconnaissance photograph analysis, intelligence work and code-breaking, among many other jobs.

Women serving in the auxiliary services sometimes manned anti-aircraft guns or searchlights, or found themselves in other, equally hazardous positions. Hundreds of women died in the defence of their country. Who can say how Britain would have fared in the war without their sacrifice?

The work of the Women's Voluntary Service for Civil Defence, known as the WVS, was equally important. It was set up in 1938, with home secretary Sir Samuel Hoare pronouncing: "As regards their civil defence functions, the minister regards the Women's Voluntary Service as occupying … much the same relationship as that of the women's auxiliary services for the armed forces of the Crown."

The work carried out by these volunteers was vital and wide-ranging. They played a huge role in the evacuation of children in 1939, collected and distributed clothing, greeted troops returning to Britain from abroad and provided food and drink during the Blitz, while bombs fell and buildings collapsed around them: 241 WVS members were killed during the Blitz. It's said one heroic member, cooking in her own kitchen, fed 1,200 victims of the bombs in one day.

There was more, much more. The WVS – more than a million of them at one time – organised incident inquiry points, where information about missing loved ones could be gathered; transported food supplies to areas badly hit by bombing; collected materials needed for the war effort; and passed on the government's advice about the need to minimise waste, and salvage everything that could possibly be useful.

The home secretary in 1943, Herbert Morrison, was astounded by some of the work the women of the WVS were carrying out. "When I hear of some of the tasks these women have undertaken it seems to me there is a touch of genius about them," he told reporters. "Take for instance the pie scheme. Under this scheme the WVS are helping to distribute a million pies and snacks each week to agricultural workers in some 2,750 villages.

"Then there is the sock-darning for the Army. I understand the WVS now darn about 38,000 pairs of socks a week for our soldiers and have lately undertaken the mending of American socks too."

The WVS is still in existence today, albeit in the guise of the Women's Royal Voluntary Service. One wonders how many pairs of socks its members would be able to darn in a week.

While the WVS was distributing pies the length and breadth of Britain, the workers of the Women's Land Army

were helping to provide the means to make them. Working on the land was one of the options open to women after conscription was introduced in 1941, and by 1944 there were 80,000 'Land Girls' toiling on the country's farms.

The Land Army was set up in 1939 as the likelihood of food shortages in the coming war hit home. If more food could be produced at home and less had to be imported, ships could be freed up for other work and fewer vessels would have to dodge U-boats in the Atlantic. In addition, many male farm workers joined the armed forces to do their bit for king and country, leaving the farming industry facing a labour shortage.

So into the breach – and into their breeches – stepped the Land Girls. History does not record how many of them sang the following song, which neatly describes their work, as they toiled:

Back to the land, we must all lend a hand.
To the farms and the fields we must go.
There's a job to be done,
Though we can't fire a gun
We can still do our bit with the hoe.
Back to the land, with its clay and its sand,
Its granite and gravel and grit,
You grow barley and wheat
And potatoes to eat
To make sure that the nation keeps fit.
We will tell you once more
You can help win the war
If you come with us – back to the land.

Naturally, all kinds of farming jobs had to be done, and the Land Girls had to learn them quickly. This was not always easily accomplished, for the women came from all walks of life and a third came from London and the big industrial cities of the north of England, where agriculture was often regarded as a mysterious occupation carried out in far-off places.

Many a Land Girl learnt how to milk a cow the hard way, and there were countless other skills to master: helping with the lambing, ploughing, lifting potatoes, looking after chickens, ditch-digging, fence-mending, helping with the harvest, threshing – even catching rats. A large number of Land

Army members felled trees or worked in sawmills, ensuring vital supplies of timber were supplied to industry.

Government posters aimed at potential recruits tended to show the more glamorous side of work on the land, but the reality was often different. For the princely sum of 32 shillings a week, Land Girls endured the worst of the British weather living either in a hostel or on the farm, which was all too often located a long way from the comforts of urban life and boasted neither hot water nor electricity.

And many new recruits must have been horrified when they were confronted by their uniforms. The Land Army was not part of the armed forces

Above:
Wrens' roles included those of mechanic, weapons analyst and radar plotter

so the wearing of a uniform was not enforced, and many a Land Girl must have been glad of that. Standard issue consisted of a khaki overcoat, brown breeches or dungarees, a green jumper and a brown felt hat. At least the overcoat would have been welcome as you broke up the hard soil with your hands in the depths of winter, and the other garments could always be altered.

An Essex woman, recalling her first day on duty in the Land Army, remembered distinctly that reality hit home hard. Told to meet a lorry at 6.30 on a winter morning, she was convinced the village clocks had been tampered with. "I had to break the ice in the water jug before washing," she said. "My oilskin crackled. It smelled of disinfectant. I wore umpteen layers of everything I could lay my hands on. I could hardly walk."

But worse was to come as she arrived at the farm with 13 other girls. "We all staggered out of the lorry, slipping in the mud and somehow stood facing an enormous sugar beet field. We had to clear it! No one had any work experience, no training.

"The foreman heaved up a sugar beet in each hand, clutching the leaves – the

Left: Land Army members were obliged to learn countless skills

beets were as big as our heads. The idea was to bang them together and toss them neatly in a row minus soil. We set off, but we nearly all sank without trace.

"Having staggered to the end of our two rows, I stood up with difficulty. I knew my back was broken and would never mend. My dad was right, I should never have left home!"

So life in the Land Army could be hard, and working conditions were sometimes very far from ideal. The maximum working week of 50 hours in the summer and 48 hours in the winter – spread over five and a half days – was often exceeded, especially when there was the harvest to get in or ewes in labour to be tended. And there is plenty of evidence to show that farmers, who were responsible for paying the Land Girls, often handed over less than the agreed rate or overcharged for board and lodging – or both.

Despite all these hardships, many Land Girls looked back on their lives down on the farm with affection. There was the rewarding feeling that they were contributing in a massively important way to the survival of their country; there was the camaraderie that built up among the women, which often

resulted in lifelong friendships; and, if all else failed, there was the Saturday night dance in the local town to be enjoyed.

Also doubtless looking forward to precious free time at the weekend were the millions of women who stepped in to take men's places in factories and other workplaces when their country needed them. Women had, of course, been employed in factories since the start of the industrial revolution, but their numbers grew dramatically after the events of September 1939.

Here Britain held a key advantage over the enemy. While British women drove the wheels of industry that kept the armed forces supplied with munitions, Hitler forbade their German counterparts to work in weapons factories: a woman's place was at home, he insisted, despite the pleas of Albert Speer, the minister for armaments and war, for workforce reinforcements. Instead, slave workers who had been captured in foreign territories helped to manufacture the weapons Germany needed so badly – and many seized the opportunity to lend Britain a helping hand by sabotaging the process.

Back in Britain, women had eagerly taken over where the menfolk had left off. The doubters were many – women couldn't do the job of a man in industry, they scoffed – but they were proved wrong: while women admittedly couldn't do the heavy lifting some jobs required, they could do pretty much everything else a man could do, and in many cases do it better.

A Ministry of Work circular to local offices early in the war warned that, in view of the shortage of women's labour in many areas, it was becoming increasingly necessary to tap potential sources of supply among women who did not normally work. It was working, it said, to bring to women's notice the need for them to volunteer for work, and it urged employers to use the services of older women and those who could only work part-time. The initiative was successful.

Despite the fact that a large proportion of them had never experienced work outside the home before the war, women adapted to the industrial life with style, and in staggering numbers. Of all the workers in the chemical and explosives industries, for example, more than half were female; more than 1.5 million women worked in the engineering and metal industries; in all, around seven million women dedicated their labour to the war effort in industry.

Out of the factories poured aircraft, tanks, munitions, uniforms, cable and wire, parachutes, barrage balloons and a thousand other products. Not that women's efforts were always appreciated to the full.

Skilled female workers were able to earn a weekly wage of about £2 in this kind of work, but the sorry fact is that men doing the same work received more. It was even fairly common for an unskilled man to earn more than a skilled woman, a fact that did not go unnoticed by the female workers of the Rolls-Royce factory in Glasgow. They went on strike in protest at the injustice.

The industrial action was seen as provocative and unpatriotic at a time when Britons were giving up their lives for their country, and a demonstration by the Rolls-Royce workers was met by a hail of eggs and tomatoes. The counter-demonstrators must have been truly enraged to sacrifice precious foodstuffs, but they calmed down when they heard how much the women were being paid. The dispute was settled and the women returned to work with a partial victory – they were to receive the same pay as a semi-skilled male worker.

A Cheshire women gave researchers a taste of what life was like for a woman working in a munitions factory. "On my first afternoon there," she said, "I was

Above: Nurses take part in a gas attack drill

Centre: Women's work in factories gave an enormous boost to the war effort

put in the experimental shop, where we had to test the powder by weighing it on brass scales and sealing detonators one at a time. We had to wear goggles and leather gauntlets.

"One day I was given a red box to carry with one person in front and one behind carrying red flags, taking it to be stored in a magazine to be used later. I didn't know what I was carrying."

There was a massive explosion, she recalled, and she dropped the box. She was shocked to see a terribly injured young woman being thrown through a window by the blast. "Luckily, the box, which contained detonators, did not explode or we would have had our legs blown off.

"I was sickened. When I got home, I said to my sisters: "I'm not going back there again." They laughed at me because they knew I had to go again."

The next day, she continued, she asked someone what detonators were like. "They must have thought I was stupid because someone said: 'Those are what you are making now.' I nearly fainted."

That woman was just one of countless thousands who put their lives in danger on the home front. Many others paid the ultimate price and perished. All of them – in factories, on the land, in

ambulances or hospitals, on fire watch or in the auxiliary services – contributed in inestimable fashion to the winning of the war. And there was another, equally significant, result of women's surge to work during the war.

Before 1939, a woman's place was at home and a man's place was at work. A woman might work if she had no family to look after, but it was generally expected that she would give up when she married or when she had her first child. That attitude was challenged with the advent of World War II.

Workplaces, too, were forced to change. Employers were obliged to consider the needs of working women and make allowance for flexible working hours, even nurseries.

With the demobilisation of the armed forces after the war, men in their millions returned to the posts they had occupied before, and women, often to their anger, found themselves out of a job. But society had changed, and new attitudes prevailed. The lesson had been learnt that women could do jobs traditionally assigned to men.

As well as defying Hitler on the home front, Britain's women had laid the foundations for those who fought – and are fighting still – for equal opportunities for women.

Above: Hitler, despite the advice of his armaments minister Albert Speer (left), forbade German women to work in arms factories

Centre: British women, and their American counterparts, worked tirelessly in the munitions factories

Digging for Victory

Never was the old proverbial saying 'necessity is the mother of invention' more apt than in Britain between 1939 and 1945. The country, hampered by reduced imports and the need to keep its population fed and its military supplied with the resources to win the war, was forced to fall back on its ingenuity, as well as sheer hard work.

Innumerable schemes, plans, projects and campaigns, the result of both public and private initiative, sprang into life as the nation dug deep – literally – to bolster the war effort. Perhaps the best remembered of these was the Dig for Victory campaign.

The government wasted little time in urging the people of Britain to dig for victory, introducing its campaign in October 1939, a month after the declaration of war. Every man and woman in the country should be encouraged to have a go at growing their own vegetables and fruit, it reasoned, even if that meant turning precious lawns and flower beds into allotments.

The minister for agriculture, Robert Hudson, proclaimed: "We want not only the big man with the plough but the little man with the spade to get busy this autumn. Let 'Dig for Victory' be the motto of everyone with a garden."

More than 10 million instructional leaflets were distributed, with the first

SPRING

WARTIME GARDENING GUIDE

WHAT TO GROW AND HOW TO GROW IT

Issued in support of
THE MINISTRY OF AGRICULTURE'S
"DIG FOR VICTORY" CAMPAIGN

by P. DYER, N.D.H., D.I.P.A.
Edited by:—
ROY HAY (of BBC "Radio Allotment"

1/6

A VICTORY LIBRARY BOOK   SERIES 1 NUMBER 1

promising "vegetables for you and your family every week of the year. Never a week without food from your garden or allotment. Not only fresh peas and lettuce in June and new potatoes in July, but all the health-giving vegetables in winter, when supplies are scarce."

It's hardly surprising, given the millions of rumbling stomachs caused by rationing, that Britons in their thousands took up their spades, forks and dibbers, rolled up their sleeves and got down to work. It is estimated that at one point more than 1.4 million allotments were being cultivated, and in 1943 they produced over a million tons of vegetables. Even tennis courts, parks and golf clubs – even the moat of the

Tower of London – were not safe from the armies of victory diggers.

Graphic artists and copywriters were busy throughout the war to keep the gardeners informed, with seasonal update leaflets and instructions on such subjects as manuring fruit trees, seedbeds and how to maintain an efficient working toolshed. Companion planting – growing different plants close to each other so that they help each other in pest control and pollination – was encouraged.

Other leaflets showed how household items that might otherwise be thrown away could be used to advantage on the allotment. Toilet paper rolls and egg cartons could be used as planters, for example; old net curtains could keep birds off the crops; and even crumbling window frames could be used to make serviceable cold frames.

The men in Whitehall worked on keeping spirits up at the same time as spreading the message, and one result was this jolly ditty:

Dig! Dig! Dig! And your muscles will grow big.
Keep on pushing the spade.
Don't mind the worms,
Just ignore their squirms,
And when your back aches laugh with glee.
And keep on diggin'
Till we give our foes a wiggin'.
Dig! Dig! Dig! To victory!

But the drive to keep the nation fed wasn't just about digging. Families were encouraged to keep chickens, while some also kept pigs, rabbits and goats.

Pigs were especially popular as they could be fed on kitchen scraps on their way to providing tasty bacon for the winter, and families often got together to form 'pig clubs', sharing the responsibilities as well as the spoils of animal husbandry.

One young lad during the war told amateur historians many years later that poultry was kept in his family's back garden to provide eggs and a cockerel for Christmas – though the "murder, plucking and disembowelment" of one of his friends inclined him towards vegetarianism at an early age. "It's not that people were cruel – necessity demanded it," he said. "We also had a pig but the end of her I leave to the imagination."

Of his father's efforts in digging for victory he remembered: "Potatoes were a staple crop along with cabbages and peas, rhubarb, celery, lettuce, runner beans, blackcurrants and leeks, and one year my Dad grew something called sweetcorn, which everybody watched come to fruition. Though it tasted nice it was eaten with some suspicion because we hadn't a clue what it really was.

"Each year the mayor or some such character came to judge the efforts of men who worked, fire-watched and

RAGS *make* . . . . UNIFORMS

METAL *makes* . . . TANKS

PAPER *makes* BULLETS

Save waste for war weapons

dug for victory. Prizes I cannot recall, but Dad had several red First Prize cards, and we got something to eat, of course."

An Edinburgh woman was another who had vivid memories of the Dig for Victory campaign, but her involvement was of a different nature. A botanist by profession, she was enlisted as a gardens allotment volunteer and used her knowledge to give advice on how to grow food. "Most folk in Edinburgh weren't gardeners, and we showed them what to do," she told the BBC's researchers. "There was a limited number of seeds and plants and I used to take some seeds from my own garden to give to people.

"To get a plot, people had to apply to the headquarters at St Andrew's House. Supplies of grass seed dried up completely at that time. It was used up to sow runways all over the place. In 1943 I went to Aberdeen and was a pioneer in working out how to store potatoes indoors because there was no wheat, so there was no straw."

The Dig for Victory message was taken on board enthusiastically all over the country, and as the war went on it became clear that its success

had even exceeded the government's expectations. But there was no room for complacency, and in 1944, despite expectations that the war would be over in a matter of months, the minister of agriculture insisted that there was still much work to be done – even after the war.

"We can justly congratulate ourselves on what we have achieved," Robert Hudson wrote. "But we must on no account relax our efforts. The war is not yet won. Moreover, even if it were to end in Europe sooner than we expect, the food situation, far from becoming easier, may well become more difficult owing to the urgent necessity of feeding the starving people of Europe.

"Indeed, in many ways it would be true to say that our real tasks will only then begin. Carry on, therefore, with your good work. Do not rest on your spades, except for those brief periods which are every gardener's privilege."

So it was that the people of Britain carried on digging for victory even after that victory had been won. Even though parks, golf courses and moats have been returned to their original purposes, some of those people are digging to this day.

Far Left: Nothing should go to waste, the people of Britain were told

So necessity proved to be the mother of invention on the British home front, and another proverb – 'waste not, want not' – proved useful when the government wanted to remind the population that every little bit helped to boost the war effort. Wastage of food or any useful material was portrayed as an act almost akin to treason.

"Make Do and Mend" became the watchword on posters and in advertisements, while other propaganda featured the nasty little Squander Bug or promoted the idea that the enemy would benefit from waste.

The Make Do and Mend campaign encouraged households to get as much wear out of their clothes – which were subject to rationing, as we have seen – as they possibly could. "Go through your wardrobe", one poster urged, as people were told to determine which garments could be used again. Evening classes were set up to teach how to make new clothes from pieces of worn-out garments, and many ingenious solutions were devised in the drive to make a little go a long way.

Old raincoats were cut up to make babies' bibs; squares were cut out of stockings to make dishcloths; the soles of children's shoes were varnished in an attempt to extend their working lives; wood surfaces were cleaned with cold tea dregs; jewellery was fashioned out of corks, bottle tops, cup hooks and other household items; egg shells were crushed and added to cleaning products to increase their scouring potential.

One woman in Cheshire recalled some clever ways of adding to the clothing ration, with 'make do and mend' to the forefront in her family's thinking. "We did a lot of 'turning'," she said. "When a coat was looking shabby, the lining was removed and washed and ironed. The coat was unpicked, washed and pressed and then sewn together inside out, the lining was replaced and it was looking almost as good as new. Dress skirts got the same treatment.

"As knitting wool was on coupons, garments that had seen better days were unravelled, the wool wrapped round a 12-inch ruler or stout cardboard, the wool steamed in front of a boiling kettle and then re-knitted."

The improvisation did not end there. "Church jumble sales were a great source of material," she recalled. "The skirt of a dress provided enough material to make a blouse, a coat unpicked and turned made a dress, skirts and jumpers unravelled and steamed took on a new identity. Curtains, like the curate's egg – good in parts – finished up as cushion covers. All this, and no coupons surrendered."

Another woman, whose mother was dressmaker, told a story of an equally resourceful use for old clothes. "Every lad in the village would have trousers made by my mum from the lower legs of his father's trousers," she said. "The legs then being much fuller, they could be cut off below the knee and each leg made one side of the trousers. Mum would then finish them off with paper buttoned flies.

"The sleeves of old cardigans would be taken out and changed over, thus placing the worn elbows in the front of the arms to prolong their lives."

Try to persuade one of today's youngsters that the sleeves of her top would have to be changed over, and wait for the reaction. The lengths to which people were prepared to go to get the most out of their wardrobes are almost unthinkable today.

Meanwhile, while nimble-fingered amateur seamstresses and tailors were fashioning new clothes from material that would today be binned, the government continued to drive home the 'waste not,

want not' message in other areas.

Squander Bug posters featured an evil-looking little green creature, dotted with Nazi swastikas, accompanying housewives on their daily shopping trips and rejoicing when they overspent in expensive shops. Other posters proclaimed: "Don't waste food – don't take more than you can eat", "A clear plate means a clear conscience" and "Better pot-luck with Churchill today than humble pie under Hitler tomorrow".

As minister of food Lord Woolton reminded listeners in a broadcast: "If you are only eating what you need and not what you like and as much as you like, then you are helping to win the war."

But the economy drive was not confined to the home. Fuel was precious, and the more that could be dedicated to military use the better. So Britons planning a train journey were confronted by Railway Executive Committee posters asking: "Is your journey really necessary?"

Others advocated the use of Shanks's pony rather than public transport – "Walk short distances and leave room for those who have longer journeys". After all, you didn't want to be branded a Transport Hog like George:

You wonder why we make a fuss
If George decides to take a bus,
But look again and you will see
That George ain't all that George should be.
He's only got a step to go,
A couple hundred yards or so,
While others further down the queue
Have far to go and lots to do.
When George gets on we often find
That other folk get left behind.
He pays his fare and rides the stage,
And off he hops, and see the rage.
And seeing this gives George a jog.
"Perhaps I'm just a Transport Hog."

George was doubtless the kind of man who left food on his plate, took the bus when he could have walked and refused to let his old clothes be recycled into boys' trousers. And he had probably never heard the word 'salvage'.

The principle of salvage formed another facet of the government's crusade to maximise the use of every single scrap of food, every household product and every material to feed the war effort. Nothing could be allowed to go to waste. Nowadays the same principle is known as 'recycling', although little thought was given in those days to man's effect on the environment; it was all about helping to win the war.

An example: one national salvage drive resulted in 70 million books being collected in the 14 months up to December 1943, the authorities announced. What use could be made of old books? They were sorted by 'scrutineers' into three categories: those that could be pulped to help in the making of munitions; those that were used to restock libraries that had been bombed; and those that went to be read by service men and women.

As ever, the salvage campaign was vigorously supported by posters, leaflets and slogans. One poster showing a cowed Führer being stuffed into a dustbin and featured the words "Help put the lid on Hitler by saving your old metal and paper." Another urged: "Save kitchen waste to feed the pigs!" and added "It also feeds poultry … your council will collect."

All over Britain, households were told to divide their salvage materials into four categories: tins and other metal, which could be used in the manufacture of aircraft and tanks; paper, which could

Help put the lid on Hitler BY SAVING YOUR OLD METAL AND PAPER

Left: Saving metal and paper could help put the lid on Hitler, a poster announced

be recycled; kitchen waste, for feeding those hungry pigs and chickens; and bones, which, after being boiled, could be used for making glue or glycerine, used in explosives.

A Shropshire woman remembered that, when she was about 10 years old, her family volunteered to do the work of a salvage depot, collecting mainly paper and card and using a big greenhouse to store it.

DIGGING FOR VICTORY

Far Right: Dornier bombers, free at last from being chased by British aircraft made from salvaged metal, including the kettle made famous in song

She continued: "We used a child's trolley and I would go all by myself to the neighbours to collect salvage from about 40 neighbouring houses. Mum would pack it all into hessian sacks. We also had a big notice on the gate saying 'salvage depot' and people would drop more stuff in. A big lorry, perhaps from the council, came round every Friday to collect it."

Scrap metal, ranging from razor blades to iron gates and railings, was collected too, which explains why so many buildings and squares were railingless after the war, and in a lot of cases still are.

"The government made some sort of order that requisitioned iron railings and gates," said a Bedfordshire man remembering the war. "The material they wanted was wrought iron but the workmen who came round with oxyacetylene cutters took every iron gate and railing in sight. These included the Victorian cast iron gates and railings from the front of a Congregational Church, as well as those that surrounded a church graveyard.

"Unfortunately, there seemed to be insufficient capacity to deal with cast iron and consequently, a pile of cast iron gates and railings could be seen in a local scrapyard until well after the war."

He went on: "There are a number of locations around the older part of the town where it is still possible to see squares or circles of lead set into the tops of walls or gateways – they have a short stump of the original railing or gate remaining. One strange thing is that these stumps do not appear to have rusted away in the 60-plus years since the cutting torch was used."

And then there was the 'Saucepans for Spitfires' initiative, under which melted-down aluminium kitchen vessels found their way into the aircraft factories. A popular song of the time went:

My saucepans have all been surrendered,
The teapot is gone from the hob.
The colander's leaving the cabbage
For a very much different job.
So now, when I hear on the wireless
Of Hurricanes showing their mettle,
I see in a vision before me
A Dornier chased by my kettle.

Every single man, woman and child in Britain, not to mention their kitchen utensils, had a hand in winning the war.

Under Threat

Far Right:
Sheltered from the
threat of air raids

Throughout the war, from the declaration of war in September 1939 until the explosion of the last V-2 rocket in Kent in March 1945, Britain was vulnerable to a multitude of threats of widely differing natures. There was, of course, the daily threat of bombing raids; there was the ever-present menace of spies and fifth columnists plying their deadly trade in the hearts of communities; and at different times there was the very real possibility of the country being invaded.

As ever, Britain's people were ready, willing and able to stand up to every one of these dangers. Preparations to repel the long-feared invasion ranged from fortification of the coastline to the training of home-based forces and the design of disinformation campaigns. Anti-air raid work went on throughout the war. And every man, woman and child was on the alert for the suspicious behaviour or unfamiliar face that might betray the presence of a spy.

We have already looked at the harsh realities of air raids, and will examine the defensive measures taken to ensure British territory remained British in the next chapter. But in this chapter there is much to be learnt about how the country and its people dealt with the threat of espionage.

The moment war was declared in 1939, there was great concern about the possible presence of German spies working within the population. After all, hadn't the government immediately interned thousands of Germans and Austrians as a preventive measure? Just as worrying was the thought that fifth columnists – Nazi sympathisers who, although British, would not hesitate to pass information to the enemy – might be at work. The government was not slow to act to counter this threat.

February 1940 saw the introduction of the Ministry of Information's Careless Talk Costs Lives campaign. Posters, many of them created by the famous *Punch* cartoonist Fougasse, appeared on walls

Above: The Keep Mum message warned Britons to remain tight-lipped

know who's on the wires! Be careful what you say."

Other posters encouraged the people to "Keep Mum – she's not so dumb." A tight-lipped but glamorous mother was portrayed surrounded by eager suitors in uniform – who could say which one of them might be a fifth columnist?

The British people, delighting in the humour, took the campaign to their hearts, and equally took the message to heart. It was short, punchy and to the point, unlike a previous slogan which had advised: "Do not discuss anything that might be of national importance. The consequence of any such indiscretion may be the loss of many lives."

Its short, sharp approach was much more like the 'seven rules' promoted by the government that pointed the way towards responsible behaviour in wartime: don't waste food; don't talk to strangers; keep all information to yourself; listen to government instructions and carry them out; report anything suspicious to police; don't spread rumours; and lock up anything that might help the enemy in the event of invasion.

The Careless Talk Costs Lives message's success in keeping a nation on

and cinema advertisements and helped to spread the message: be careful who you talk to and be just as careful what you say.

Many of the posters had a humorous slant, often featuring a disguised Hitler listening in on thoughtless pieces of gossip, on a train or in a café. In one, a monstrous Führer was balanced precariously on some telephone wires with his hand cupped to his ear while the slogan reminded readers: "You never

LITTLE BOOK OF **BRITAIN AT WAR**

its toes was outstanding and, although the number of real spies in Britain was in reality very small, there were some spectacular results when culprits were caught. One story was recounted by a Newcastle upon Tyne woman to the BBC's People's War researchers.

Her family, she remembered, provided a billet for a Canadian WRAF woman called Trixie, who quickly became part of the family. She didn't socialise with any local RAF staff but often travelled far afield, to Birmingham, Leeds and Glasgow – she had work to do and friends to visit, she explained. Trixie regularly received letters and parcels – containing nylons for the mother, sweets and chewing gum for the children – which she said were from her brother.

"I don't know how my mother became suspicious, but she did," said the Newcastle woman, "and one night, after Trixie had been to Coventry the previous night, that city was hammered by the Luftwaffe. She visited Bristol and then Liverpool with similar consequences.

"At this stage my mother took into her confidence the ex-detective living nearby. He suggested she stay up and await Trixie's return. The lady who let herself in was unrecognisable to my

Don't forget that walls have ears!

CARELESS TALK COSTS LIVES

mother – long black hair, very well made-up features, etc. When asked to explain, she said she had been with friends to a wonderful fancy dress party!"

It was later found that a trunk in Trixie's bedroom had a false bottom, concealing wigs, stage make-up and clothes – and the letters she had been receiving from her 'brother' in Canada were written in German and had been sent by her controller to Canada and

Above: German spy Karel Richter is interviewed in the field where he landed

thence to England.

"My sister and I were sent into the garden while her arrest was made," recalled the woman. "I remember so clearly one of the loveliest dolls I had ever owned being bundled, along with all the other gifts Trixie had brought, into the coke boiler by my parents. Much later in life, I understood."

While Trixie proved to be a real spy, other tales of the unveiling of espionage, while doubtless sincere, were built on rather less solid foundations. One, which has echoes of the popular wartime scare story about German parachutists descending on Britain dressed as nuns, was told by a Bedford man. His father,

he said, was at the railway station one day when he noticed a couple of nuns on the platform. "They appeared to be wandering about pointing their umbrellas at the railway sidings and the local munitions factory.

"My father was suspicious and so alerted the station supervisor, who in turn alerted the authorities. The 'nuns' were arrested. It turned out that they were indeed German spies checking out potential targets."

Some German spies did indeed parachute into the country, although not disguised as nuns. One such was Karel Richter. His espionage mission did not last long.

Richter, who had previously tried to escape from Germany, had bought his release from a concentration camp by agreeing to spy for his fatherland. In May 1941 he was told to parachute into England, pass some equipment to a fellow spy, determine whether the other man was a double agent – entirely possible given Britain's superb record in 'turning' captives – and gather information on the lie of the land.

Richter's mission did not get off to a good start. After hiding for two days without food he felt very ill and, seeking help, strayed onto a road in Hertfordshire, where two lorry drivers found him. The drivers, noticing that he seemed to be foreign, pointed him out to a police constable doing his rounds, and at the local police station it was found that Richter was carrying £551 in British notes and 1,400 American dollars – enormous sums to be wandering around with.

The military intelligence agency MI5 was soon involved and Richter confessed his guilt. When the field in which he had landed was searched, a radio transmitter, a pistol and a torch were found. Karel Richter was executed for espionage, at the age of 29, on 10 December.

So there were success stories resulting from the British people's constant vigilance in the hunt for spies and fifth columnists. But the public's essential contribution in cases like that of Karel Richter did not diminish the government's determination to keep the country on permanent alert, as a wireless broadcast later in the war showed.

However great the success in detecting enemy agents, Britons should never assume that the menace had been eradicated, listeners heard.

Modern methods of transport and communication made the spy's job easier. The broadcast continued: "While we have been glad to welcome to our country many thousands of genuine refugees from Nazi oppression, the presence of so many foreign subjects in our midst can only make the detection of the spy more difficult.

"Whereas an English accent heard in the streets of Berlin might immediately betray the presence of a British agent, a foreign tongue spoken in Britain today does not even call for comment. It is therefore a most important duty for all of us to make the work of the enemy spy, who may be present in the country, as

difficult as possible."

Once again, the British people were told never to discuss any subject likely to be of interest to the enemy in a public place. "You may look round quickly and say to yourself, 'Oh, it's all right, we're all friends here'," the broadcast went on. "Or you may say, 'Well there's no harm in talking about that here, because everybody here knows about it.' But are you quite sure there are no strangers present?"

So the Careless Talk Costs Lives and Keep Mum messages continued to be hammered home.

Meanwhile, there were other broadcasters keen to get the attention of the people of Britain, and persuade them that the cause they were promoting was the right one. These broadcasters never entered a BBC studio, however; they transmitted their twisted propaganda from Hamburg, in northern Germany.

Lord Haw-Haw was the derisive nickname most usually given by British listeners to William Joyce, an Irish-American fascist politician who broadcast mocking and threatening accounts of heavy Allied losses, the sinking of ships and the shooting down of aircraft. In fact, the programme *Germany Calling*, transmitted on shortwave radio by the Reichssender Hamburg station under the control of propaganda minister Joseph Goebbels, had several announcers,

of which Joyce was just one. But the nickname stuck most readily to Joyce.

The broadcasts, whether made by Joyce or by one of his cohorts, aimed to demoralise both the armed forces and those on the home front and persuade them that the Nazis would inevitably triumph. They had willing listeners in Britain for, despite their ridiculous and irritating claims about Allied losses, they also contained information about servicemen who had not come back from bombing raids, or who were otherwise missing. Information like this – even though possibly false – was eagerly sought by anxious loved ones.

So the nation, or at least part of it, listened in to Lord Haw-Haw intoning his trademark "Germany calling, Germany calling," and was amused, disgusted and comforted in equal measure by what followed. Then, on 30 May 1945, British forces over-ran Hamburg and the broadcasts ceased.

William Joyce was shot as he tried to escape arrest near the German border with Denmark, but that did not prevent him being transported to England, where he was put on trial. The fact that he could be said to be a subject of King George VI because of his British passport – to which, ironically, he was not entitled – allowed him to be convicted of treason.

He was hanged at Wandsworth Prison on 3 January 1946. Lord Haw-Haw had been silenced.

Centre:
Goebbels' domain
– the Propaganda
Ministry building in
Berlin

Defence of the Realm

O n the evening of Tuesday, 14 May 1940, just as they had done the previous September, British families throughout the land were once again gathered around their wireless sets. The word had gone out that Anthony Eden, secretary of state for war, was going to make an important announcement regarding the future conduct of the war.

To put it simply, prospects were bleak for Britain at that point. They had seldom been bleaker. A few days previously, the Wehrmacht and Luftwaffe, the Germans' ground and air forces, had launched their deadly blitzkrieg on Belgium and the Netherlands, and had swept away all the resistance they met. The evacuation of the British Expeditionary Force from

Dunkirk in northern France was a few days away, and that would leave the white cliffs of Dover within range of the Nazi commanders. Britain was staring invasion full in the face.

Eden began to speak, and the families, especially the men, listened intently. "I want to speak to you tonight about a form of warfare which the Germans have been employing so extensively against Holland and Belgium," he said. "We are going to ask you to help in a manner which I know will be welcome to thousands of you."

Eden was coming to the part the men wanted to hear. "The government has received enquiries from all over the kingdom from men who wish to

do something for the defence of the country," he continued. "Now is your opportunity.

"We want large numbers of such men … to come forward now and offer their services. The name of the new force will be the Local Defence Volunteers. In order to volunteer, what you have to do is to give in your name at your local police station …"

In the first episode of the BBC's *Dad's Army*, these words were the cue for an achingly funny scene as swarms of men of all ages, sizes, professions and dispositions besieged the Walmington-on-Sea police station, with bank manager George Mainwaring crushed against the counter at the front. As always in the classic Home Guard sitcom, the scriptwriters had grabbed the chance of a little comedic exaggeration, but their gags were based firmly on reality.

After just six days, a quarter of a million men had come forward to join the Local Defence Volunteers. By mid-July, with the Battle of Britain about

Above: Anthony Eden announced the formation of the Local Defence Volunteers in 1940

Centre: Home Guard in training with a Blacker Bombard spigot mortar

to erupt in the skies above their heads, their number had swollen to 1.3 million. By the middle of November, another 400,000 had joined the ranks.

By that time, the LDV had been renamed the Home Guard. A valuable fighting force and a much-loved institution had been born.

The Home Guard owed its existence in large part to the work of Captain Tom Wintringham, a veteran of World War I and the Spanish Civil War. While in Spain he had learnt invaluable lessons in guerrilla warfare and determined to put them to use should the need arise

in Britain. Wintringham set up a school in guerrilla tactics in west London and, once the LDV had been formed, set about training thousands of men.

But Wintringham's work, although credited with raising the morale and effectiveness of many volunteers, was never officially recognised – there were suspicions about his political leanings – and his school was taken over by the government after three months. His training model was followed, however, and adapted at other centres established throughout the country.

Much official thought had been given to the idea of locally-based home defence

forces, and some individuals had even taken the initiative and formed their own private groups. The government's hand was forced by public pressure and by 13 May, the day before Eden's broadcast, there was some kind of plan in place. History does not record whether it was written on the back of an envelope.

But the volunteers came forward in their thousands. They were men between the ages of 17 and 65 who, for one reason or another, were not in military service but wanted to help defend their country in the event of an invasion.

Yes, they probably ranged, as in *Dad's Army*, from callow, muffler-wearing bank clerks to elderly undertakers. Yes, they were sometimes older than the prescribed 65 or younger than 17. No, they weren't always the fittest members of society – Eden had made it clear that as long as you were capable of free movement, you were welcome to enlist.

In truth, the early months of the LDV were something of a shambles. The government's intentions were worthy and a great deal of work went into setting up the necessary local organisations, but in the summer of 1940 there were other pressing matters eating up the officials' time and resources. The need to evacuate more than 300,000 French and

DEFENCE OF THE REALM

Right: Wartime Prime Minister Winston Churchill, whose intervention helped to turn the Home Guard into a formidable fighting force

British soldiers from Dunkirk was just one of them.

As the unkindly bestowed nickname of the LDV – Look, Duck and Vanish – became common currency, frustration was building among the volunteers. War Office resources were being directed elsewhere, and instead of uniforms they received LDV armbands; there were no real arms and at first volunteers were trained in the use of Molotov cocktails and other improvised weapons. Many an LDV man patrolled the streets and airfields armed with his own pitchfork, shotgun, golf club or vintage rifle 'commandeered' from the local museum. Many a steel plate was added to a private vehicle in an attempt to produce an armoured car. Many a World War I pistol was taken out of a drawer, cleaned, oiled and polished and taken on patrol.

It's little wonder that the enemy's reaction to these first stumbling efforts at forming a home defence force was derisive. Nazi propaganda minister Joseph Goebbels sneeringly called the LDV a 'rabble' and 'a mob of amateurs armed with broomsticks and darts'. He wasn't too far from the truth, for once in his life.

But change was on the way, and it

was stemming from a man who was no stranger to stirring things up. Prime minister Winston Churchill, dismayed by the low morale and discipline displayed by the LDV, insisted that the despised armbands be discarded and the name of the force changed to Home Guard.

And as the war dragged on, with the threat of invasion first looming then receding, the Home Guard grew to become a truly fearsome, revered fighting force.

First they received proper uniforms, then weapons, including rifles donated by the American National Rifle Association. Training, following the example set by Tom Wintringham, improved by leaps and bounds. The Home Guard was given weapons, such as anti-tank mortars, that the army no longer needed, and the standard of other weaponry improved beyond measure.

And the weapons were often fired in anger. Although the threatened invasion – which was to be signalled by the ringing of church bells and use of the code word Oliver – never took place, the Home Guard had plenty of practice in engaging the enemy. Besides their regular patrols and lookout duties, some members manned their own anti-aircraft weapons and delighted in taking down numerous Luftwaffe aircraft and V-2 rockets. Others took charge of artillery batteries on the coasts, and some even took on the Luftwaffe's finest with machine guns.

It's often assumed, nevertheless, that the work of the Home Guard member was a bit of a cushy number and free from real danger. How wrong can you be? A total of 1,206 men were killed while on duty and another 557 seriously wounded.

From 1942 onwards the Home Guard was not merely a volunteer force, either. The National Service Act permitted compulsory enrolment of members where a unit was below strength. At this point, the lowest rank was changed from 'volunteer' to 'private'.

Nor should it be forgotten that these men – many women carried out support work but were not permitted to take on combat roles – worked full-time during the day before assuming their Home Guard duties at night. And those duties were often not of a light nature.

If you were not patrolling stations, beaches, factories, rivers or airfields on the lookout for aircraft or parachutists, you might be building anti-tank defences or concrete pillbox guard posts, erecting barbed wire barriers, disarming unexploded bombs or training, training again and then training some more.

In the *Home Guard Handbook*, published in 1941, the duties of volunteers were clearly laid out. Members had to guard important points; observe and report, promptly and precisely; launch an immediate attack on small, lightly armed parties of the enemy; and defend roads, villages, factories and vital points in towns in order to block enemy movement.

The handbook was also clear about what each and every member of the Home Guard had to know: every square inch of his own district; the personnel of his detachment; the headquarters of his detachment and where he was to report for duty in the event of an alarm; what the alarm signal was; and the form of reports concerning enemy landings or approaches, what the reports should contain and to whom they should be sent.

No cushy number, and just what you wanted after a hard day at the office or factory, you might think, yet those volunteered hours were gladly and readily given.

One south coast Home Guard man told researchers that his twice-weekly tour of duty ended at 6am. When he was stood down he would cycle home for a quick breakfast and ablutions and then start out for another day's work at 8am.

But despite the danger of being pounded by heavy artillery from across the Channel, it wasn't always serious stuff. Our man recalled one occasion when his platoon's jealously guarded Lewis machine gun was pressed into action.

"One summer evening a German Dornier bomber with a wisp of smoke issuing from one of its engines came limping quite low over the hill in its desperation to reach the French coast. Although I considered it to be out of range for the Lewis gun, my excited compatriots wanted some action, so I opened fire.

"I should mention that my intervention was no hindrance to the progress of the aircraft – it was in fact too far away. But we did score a ricochet or two off the spire of a nearby school. I would hazard a guess that the locals would have been wondering just whose side we were on that evening."

Another Home Guard man from

Above: Pillboxes, from which defenders could engage invaders, sprang up in strategic positions

serious danger of being skewered to the tree by a bayonet when he pulled off his balaclava to reveal himself as the local vicar (who suffered from a serious stammer).

"It was never clear why the vicar was in the wood at night, but since by that stage in the war the Home Guard was using the church hall as their headquarters, it was probably diplomatic not to enquire."

As we've seen, however, the Home Guard was far from being all beer, skittles and hooded vicars. It was a formidable defensive force, and Nazi leaders were forced to change their opinions of its capabilities from Goebbels' dismissive 'mob of amateurs' remark to a far more serious assessment. But the feared invasion never did materialise, so the true ground-fighting ability of the Home Guard was never tested to the full. 'Dad's Army' was stood down on 3 December 1944 and disbanded on the last day of 1945.

The memories and the stories remain, but there is one aspect of the Home Guard that few people knew about at the time or remember today – it acted as a cover for a top-secret force of guerrilla troops highly trained to form an effective resistance network should Germany ever invade.

Hertfordshire recalled that, working on the assumption that German invaders would find it difficult to pronounce the letter W, the password of 'Wendell Wilkie' (American president Roosevelt's ambassador-at-large) was demanded of anyone challenged by guards or patrols.

"On one occasion," he continued, "my dad and a colleague, while patrolling at night in woodland near a church, spotted a suspicious figure flitting to and fro between the trees. After a good deal of 'halting' and 'who goes there-ing', they pinned the hooded figure to a tree and invited him to say 'Wendell Wilkie'.

"He tried unsuccessfully to oblige but proved to be quite unable to say these, or indeed any other words, and was in

Above: Some pillboxes could still be seen many years after the war

Winston Churchill takes much of the credit for the formation of the Auxiliary Units. In July 1940 he wrote: "The regular defences require supplementing with guerrilla-type troops, who will allow themselves to be over-run and who thereafter will be responsible for hitting the enemy in the comparatively soft spots behind zones of concentrated attack."

To take on the important task of organising Britain's resistance, Churchill appointed major-general Colin Gubbins, who had picked up immense knowledge of guerrilla warfare during various campaigns. Gubbins asked Major John Forbes to visit Home Guard commanders and find their best men. Forbes's idea of persuading men to step forward was to deliver the sentence: "I want volunteers for a very dangerous job."

And dangerous it certainly would have been if Germany had ever invaded. The men, picked for their local knowledge and ability to live off the land, were trained to operate out of brick and concrete operational bases built 15 feet into the ground that allowed the men to vanish into the countryside. Also on the training menu were sabotage, demolition, unarmed combat and assassination.

It's said that men of the Auxiliary Units – there were 3,500 of them – were expected to operate for about two weeks before being either captured, killed by the enemy, shot by his own colleagues in the event of being wounded, or swallowing a

DEFENCE OF THE REALM

suicide pill. But in those two weeks behind enemy lines they would be capable of wreaking havoc.

Collaborators with the enemy would receive no mercy. "We had authority, if we found collaborators in any village around us, to kill them," remembered one Auxiliary Unit member. And the men were instructed to ignore German reprisals taken against local people as a result of their actions.

The Auxiliary Units were supported by Special Duty Sections, recruited from among local populations, who would identify German vehicles and officers and gather intelligence, and the whole network would be linked nationwide by a sophisticated signals structure.

Not surprisingly, given the fact that all members of the Auxiliary Units were obliged to sign the Official Secrets Act, not many reminiscences of its work exist. Few British people knew exactly what was going on in their midst.

Much easier to spot, especially if you happened to live on the south or east coast of England, were the gun batteries, fortifications and other obstacles to German invasion that sprang up in vulnerable areas.

Minefields were laid on beaches, behind which masses of barbed wire would extend for miles. Piers, which would have been useful to the enemy looking for somewhere to land, were blocked or destroyed. Tank barriers consisting of lofty assemblies of scaffolding or concrete cubes were placed carefully. Thousands of miles of anti-tank ditches were dug. Pillboxes, from where defenders could spot and shoot at invaders, were sited all over the country. And countless other measures were taken.

Among them were less obvious methods of slowing the enemy's progress, designed to confuse and misinform – although it must be said they often confused and misinformed the people of Britain too. Signposts and railway station nameplates were removed, as were petrol pumps near the coasts, and cement was applied to milestones in order to obscure the lettering.

As we saw earlier, getting lost in wartime Britain was a frequent occurrence, thanks to the blackout. With the loss of signposts and other roadside aids to navigation, finding your way around often proved difficult in daytime too. In truth, this caused as much merriment as it did annoyance. But there were other, precious ways of finding entertainment during Britain's darkest hours.

Merrie England

If every day is filled with the struggle to feed and clothe a family on slim rations, worrying about loved ones fighting overseas and anxiety over the next lethal threat to come from Germany, you tend to take your leisure time seriously. That's if you have any leisure time.

The people on the British home front grasped every opportunity to lighten the daily grind with a daily ration of escape, in whatever form they could find it. Whether it was on the radio, in the local dancehall, in the cinema or theatre or on the gramophone, Britons rejoiced in their entertainment.

The government realised that keeping the population entertained was essential in maintaining morale, especially at those times when the war was at a crisis point – during the Dunkirk evacuation or the dark hours of the Blitz and the Battle of Britain, for example.

But the vital role that this kind of escape could play was at first a lesson still be to be learnt by the government, which ordered the closure of places of entertainment in 1939, fearing they could be easy, mass-casualty targets for German bombers. Happily, there was a rapid about-turn and the cinemas and theatres reopened within weeks.

The radio, and specifically the BBC, were essential tools for the government in wartime Britain. Listened to eagerly in just about every household in the land, it was used to pass on crucial information and advice as well as bolster morale with a well-timed rallying speech by Winston Churchill or one of his colleagues. And the country's radio entertainers also helped to keep spirits up.

The most popular radio show of the war years by far was known to the nation as *ITMA – It's That Man Again*. The man in question was comedian Tommy Handley and the show's catchphrases and hilarious plotlines kept the audience in stitches from 1939 until 1949, when Handley died. At times during its run, as many as four out of ten people in Britain tuned into each broadcast.

Handley played the 'minister of aggravation and mysteries' at the Office of Twerps – you can see the way scriptwriter Ted Kavanagh's mind was working – and the cast's gentle mockery of the government went down a storm with an audience who were accustomed to endless rules and regulations imposed by Whitehall.

Listeners came to know and love characters like Colonel Chinstrap, Mrs Mopp the office char (cleaner),

and Funf the German agent. Catchphrases such "Can I do you now, sir?", "I don't mind if I do", "I go, I come back" and "After you, Claude. No, after you, Cecil" were repeated in millions of homes and workplaces.

Scripts were often based on the news of the day and modern day audiences listening to *ITMA* would be puzzled. Even Kavanagh, speaking in 1949 just as the show was finishing, said: "I myself cannot now understand some of the jokes. They were skits on ... a headline of that day's paper, and dead the following week."

But *ITMA* was adored in its time, as was Handley, who achieved the status of a national hero. When he died he was accorded the honour of two memorial services – one at St Paul's Cathedral in London, the other in his native Liverpool – and the six-mile route of his funeral cortege was lined by thousands of fans. The role Handley played in keeping the nation in good humour cannot be overstated. As *ITMA* character Mona Lott often said: "It's keeping cheerful as keeps me going".

Another more than useful tool for the government during the war was the cinema. In the days before widespread television ownership, the only visual means of keeping up with the progress of the war was via the newsreels of Pathé, which formed an important part of every cinema visit. And the Ministry of Information was not averse to insisting that its version of events was the one the public saw and believed.

Just as Lord Haw-Haw, in his broadcasts from Hamburg, inflated the number of Allied planes shot down on their sorties over Nazi territory, so Pathé reported an exaggerated toll of Luftwaffe aircraft destroyed in the Battle of Britain. And that's just one example of how morale was sustained during the bad times.

But cinema-goers also watched the multitude of public information films the government screened during the war; it was an ideal medium for broadcasting the messages officialdom needed the population to hear. A famous example was the Ministry of Information's dramatic short *Miss Grant Goes to the Door*, in which the elderly heroine follows government advice to the letter – lock maps away, immobilise your vehicle, get strangers to speak English – and captures a German spy.

Not many people went to the cinema purely to watch government propaganda, of course. They were there to see the film stars of the day in the romances, war dramas and thrillers that set their pulses racing. Even in these movies, though, there was room for more than a little patriotism.

While Hollywood stars continued to enjoy huge box office figures, the patriotic mood of the time ensured that homegrown talent was also encouraged to bloom. The careers of British stars like Tommy Handley and singer Vera Lynn benefited enormously from their film appearances, and another artist who received a massive boost from his movie roles was Tommy Trinder.

The son of a London tram driver, Trinder was a popular comedian before the war started, but signing to Ealing Studios for a few wartime films secured his reputation as one of the nation's favourite funny

men. His appearance in the 1940's *Sailors Three*, in which the comic trio find they've strayed onto a Nazi warship, and requisition it for British purposes, ensured audiences went away laughing and full of the bulldog spirit. Incidentally, further down the *Sailors Three* cast list were the unmistakable features of John Laurie, later to achieve TV immortality as Private Frazer in *Dad's Army*.

Trinder was more than an engaging comic actor. He had won the affections of audiences working his way up through music hall and revues with the rapid patter of a born stand-up comedian, memorable catchphrases – "You lucky people" among them – and an ever-present trilby hat and trademark cheeky leer.

Another comedian with a plethora of catchphrases was the Cheeky Chappie, Max Miller, whose risqué stage act filled theatres. He wasn't considered the right material for wartime films of derring-do, but he certainly made audiences forget their worries for a while. Unsurprisingly given the saucy nature of his act, Miller never found a niche in television either, but as he used to

Right: The fare on offer at British cinemas during the war included the Ealing Studios production Went the Day Well?

say: "You can't help liking him."

Which could also be said of the diminutive, bespectacled comedian Arthur Askey, a star on radio before the war who went on to feature heavily in the morale-boosting films that came streaming out of British studios during the war. Among his movie roles were those of an unemployed entertainer during the Blitz in *I Thank You* and the head of an escort agency in *Miss London Ltd*.

One of Askey's co-stars in *Miss London Ltd* was Anne Shelton, a vocalist who became known for her dedication to entertaining both those on the home front and those stationed on military bases. Such was her popularity that she was offered her own radio programme, *Calling Malta*, which stayed on the air for five years.

Shelton was the first British singer to record a version of *Lili Marlene*, a love song of German origin that became just as popular with Allied troops as it was with those on the opposite side. And she was delighted to accept a rare invitation to sing with the most celebrated musical ensemble of the war years: the Glenn Miller Orchestra.

Trombonist, composer, arranger and leader of the big band that bore his name, Glenn Miller could do no wrong in the eyes of the millions who heard his hits on the radio and danced to them at a thousand Saturday night dances.

Swing was the thing, and Miller's stream of hits seemed endless: *Moonlight Serenade*, *In the Mood*, *Chattanooga Choo Choo*, *Tuxedo Junction*, *Little Brown Jug*, *Pennsylvania 6-5000*, *A String of Pearls*, *(I've Got a Gal in) Kalamazoo*, *American Patrol* … they just kept coming, and British audiences were glad. They couldn't get enough of the former farm boy from Iowa. There were also a good few Miller movies to keep the fans happy.

Farm boy turned into soldier boy. Although he was too old to serve, Miller was accepted into the American forces and played a major part in keeping the troops entertained in France and elsewhere. It was during a flight from Bedford to France that his aeroplane disappeared over the English Channel. Miller was gone, but his music lived on.

Nowhere more so than in the dancehalls, where local bands would do their best to emulate Miller's sound. The influence of the dancehalls in keeping Britain's spirits up cannot be overestimated.

A Teesside man told the BBC's People's War researchers that every town or village had a hall suitable for dancing. The bigger halls boasted orchestras while the smaller ones had a three-piece band, records or sometimes just a piano.

"Any kind of footwear would do," he continued, "but some had dancing pumps and others wore what they had, down to hobnail boots – this would be frowned on if it was a polished floor. Most people could dance, after a fashion, and get round the room without crippling their partners for life; well, usually.

"The lights, the music and the company let you forget the misery, austerity and danger of the war for a few short hours. You could live your dreams in a make-believe world on a par with a Hollywood film."

One British artist with a Hollywood connection was singer, actress and comedienne Gracie Fields, a huge star of the pre-war period who was forced to sit out most of World War

II in Santa Monica, California. Her husband, Monty Banks, was an Italian citizen who would have been interned if the couple had lived in Britain, and they were urged to go to America by Winston Churchill.

But the Rochdale lass made the occasional return to her native land to perform in army bases and factories, where her best-known song, *Sally*, always received a rapturous reception.

But the two theme songs of World War II vintage that capture the atmosphere of those years more perfectly than any other are *We'll Meet Again* and *The White Cliffs of Dover*, sung by the Forces' Sweetheart, Vera Lynn.

Dame Vera, as she was dubbed in recognition of the sterling work she had carried out for her country, was named servicemen's favourite musical performer during the Phoney War, and she went on to become a superstar, Britain's biggest female entertainer. Via her radio programme, *Sincerely Yours,* she ensured messages from loved ones to troops fighting abroad reached their destinations, and her biggest hits expressed an optimism that the public could not resist.

She acted in a trio of patriotic films and performed for the troops in theatres of war like India and Burma, but it is for her songs of hope that she was – and remains – best known.

We'll Meet Again and *The White Cliffs of Dover* will forever be linked with World War II, but it is fitting to close this book with a lyric from another Vera Lynn song that inspired millions who sustained and, in their own way, fought for Britain on the home front.

There'll always be an England,
And England shall be free,
If England means as much to you
As England means to me.

The author is grateful to the contributors to the BBC's WW2 People's War for their permission to reproduce some of their stories. WW2 People's War is an online archive of wartime memories contributed by members of the public and gathered by the BBC. The archive can be found at: bbc.co.uk/ww2peopleswar.

ALSO AVAILABLE IN THE LITTLE BOOK SERIES

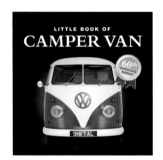

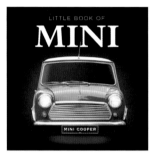

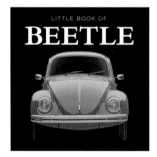

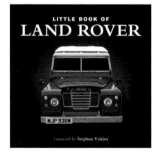

ALSO AVAILABLE IN THE LITTLE BOOK SERIES

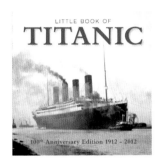

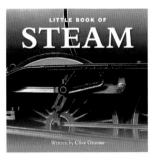

The pictures in this book were provided courtesy of the following:

WIKIMEDIA COMMONS

Design & Artwork: SCOTT GIARNESE

Published by: DEMAND MEDIA LIMITED & G2 ENTERTAINMENT LIMITED

Publishers: JASON FENWICK & JULES GAMMOND

Written by: PAT MORGAN